Bedford's Lost Children

Brenda Fraser-Newstead

First edition, 2023

To JED
the intrepid explorer

and to young people everywhere,
I wish them happiness, security, love
and a long life filled with joy.

And also
with gratitude to the memory of

MAURICE NICHOLSON
(1956 - 2022)

who contributed so much to this publication.

ISBN: 978-1-916604-06-3

Previous publications include the *Bedfordshire's Yesteryears* series comprising

Volume 1 : The Family, Childhood and Schooldays, 1993
Volume 2 : The Rural Scene, 1994
Volume 3 : Craftsmen and Trades People, 1995
Volume 4 : War Times and Civil Matters, 1996
The World Outside, 2014 – Alice May Cogan
The Ever-beckoning Byways, 2016 – Alice May Cogan

Front cover image: Embankment scene, from 'Bedfordshire Illustrated'.
Courtesy of Bedford Library https://virtual-library.culturalservices.net

INTRODUCTION

My research began when I became associated with The Friends of Bedford Cemetery, the first public cemetery in Bedford, opened on 5 June 1855. Following the opening of the Norse Road Cemetery in 1987 Bedford Cemetery was renamed Foster Hill Road Cemetery. Much has been written about notable figures interred in the Victorian cemetery and I therefore made it my purpose to research the deaths of children – from birth to age seventeen – interred in the grounds, many without a memorial, whose deaths occurred during the reign of Queen Victoria. I was curious to know the circumstances of their deaths and the more I learned the more determined I became to reveal details of the deaths of these poor little souls. Obviously, there were children who lost their lives after contracting childhood illnesses, but many died in tragic circumstances and accidental incidents. A whole generation of young people died unnecessarily through accidents whilst at play or at work and whilst reading of their demise one gains insights into the times and lives of the ordinary people of Bedford and surrounds during this progressive period of the nineteenth century – a time of Empire.

Much of my information was gleaned from local newspapers of the time and it is thanks to those Editors and Reporters that such records still exist. I have reproduced many of the articles in the same language and terminology, with explanation where necessary, for your edification [edify: to instruct or improve] as I feel it lends authenticity to the times in which it was written and published. Where clarification is obviously required, I have added my own comments. I believe the language of the time and the details given are an indication of life and death as perceived in the eighteen-hundreds. What is important is relating an awareness of these poor, unfortunate and innocent children whose lives were tragically and cruelly cut short.

Such were the hazards of life at the time that it must be the case that many children who survived to adulthood were inevitably lost in battle in the First World War. The memorials in Foster Hill Road Cemetery to the fallen no doubt bear witness to that.

Brenda Fraser-Newstead

ABOUT THE AUTHOR

 Brenda Fraser-Newstead spent many years in the world of commerce and has been a teacher, author and examiner of Business Studies, and a company director. In recent years, however, she has forsaken that involvement and found rewarding work in social welfare and the teaching of children with special needs. She originates from Wheathampstead in Hertfordshire, but her father was a Lutonian, born in the Old Bedford Road of Luton. Brenda has lived in a variety of homes in Australia, North Africa, Suffolk and finally back in Bedfordshire where she has finally found her 'dream home' and the inspiration for this her seventh book.

ACKNOWLEDGEMENTS

The author wishes to thank members of The Friends of Foster Hill Road Cemetery and staff at Bedford Central Library for the use of their facilities and for their encouragement. In particular the following deserve special mention for their expertise and assistance in research and the quest for information and guidance generally:

Maurice Nicholson
Linda Ayres
Colin Woolf
Sue Parsons
Selena Evans
Marc Nicholson

and last but not least, Jacqueline Tobin for so very professionally launching this publication.

CONTENTS

RIVER OUSE INCIDENT 26 APRIL 1879

John Fraser Handford

It was a fine Saturday afternoon in April 1879 when a happy group of friends and relatives gathered at Mr Goatley's boatyard near Bedford bridge to collect their hire boat for an excursion down the River Ouse. This was not the first time they had ventured onto the water and although the water level was high they set off at about 3pm with confidence, seating themselves comfortably in the craft.

The party consisted of five siblings, an aunt and two of the friends they had known since their time in India, where all five children were born. There were two sisters, Amy Handford aged 13 and Jane (known as Janie) Handford 11, who took the oars; there were a pair of sculls on board for the purpose of propelling the craft. Brothers Walter Handford aged 14, William Handford 16 and John Handford, 9, the youngest of the family and a pupil at Bedford Grammar School, were present, along with an aunt, Amy Walton 27. Their friends were Gerard Burge, master of a school near Maidenhead, and his younger brother Hubert Burge, who resided with their mother at 18 St Peters Street; the related group resided with their mother, the widowed Mrs Jane A Handford, at Oakfield Lodge in Kimbolton Road. The children's father, The late Mr William Handford, had been Director of Public Instruction, Oudh, and he and the Late Mr Burge, father of

Gerard and Hubert had lived together in India at one time. The friendship between both families began when they all lived in Lucknow, India.

Hire Boats

All went well as Amy and Jane rowed the considerable distance from Bedford bridge but on the approach to Castle Mill, Goldington, they wisely changed places with their aunt and brother Walter, to prepare for the return journey. In the process of changing over and as they neared a hazardous part of the river [which has been developed over time into a narrow lock and a very wide weir], the boat drifted in the strong undercurrents and the occupants lost control. They were seen to be about ten yards from the flood gates at this time. They had successfully carried out this manoeuvre only a few days earlier but on this occasion were unaware that the boat was being carried forward.

It was seen by witnesses being broadside on to the [presumably sluice-] gates [capable of being raised, thus allowing some water to be released and channelled in order to bypass the mill] and so they were 'swept onto the gates at which the waste water is discharged and when [the boat] came into collision with the wall Hubert Burge managed to jump onto the bank. Because of the proximity to the bank [and wall] it was not possible to row and the boat crashed against the archway [leading under the mill], capsized and was smashed.' It seems all of the occupants were ejected into the water and were swept down under the gates and over a ledge some four feet deep, into the mill pit and under the arch.

Six were rescued by the use of ropes and the assistance of Thomas Allen, a mill worker and witness to the accident. Sadly John who could not swim, was carried away down the stream some considerable distance away from the scene of the accident. On visiting this point only recently, the Writer noted that the water level was approximately 15 feet with the possibility of rising even higher. It was Mr Josier, a shepherd, who saw an arm around one of the 'staunches' about three-quarters of an hour after the incident; he noted that the head was about three inches under the water. The distance between the mill and the staunch was said to be two or three hundred yards. Three other men were called to help pull the little boy's body from the water and lay it in the Cople meadow until the police arrived. PC Stockbridge assisted to remove the body to the Swan Inn, Goldington.

An inquest was held at the Swan Inn, Goldington on Monday 28 April 1879, before Mr M Whyley, coroner, and a jury of thirteen members was sworn in. Mr Robert Kinsay, Bedford surgeon, who had examined the body, concluded by stating that the 'immediate cause of death was suffocation.'

The jury returned a verdict of 'Accidentally drowned'. At the close of the inquiry Mr William B Walton, the grandfather of the Handford children, entered the proceedings to make a case for action to be taken to prevent accidents in the future. After some discussion it was suggested by Mr Horrell that a public notice should be erected warning people of the danger. This suggestion met with the approval of the coroner and all the jury, who expressed a desire that this was done. Following the inquest, the child's body was taken to his home in Kimbolton Road to remain in the drawing room awaiting the funeral at Bedford Cemetery.

The funeral took place on Wednesday 30 April 1879 at Bedford Cemetery, when the coffin was conveyed on a handsome funeral car, followed by firstly a carriage drawn by a pair of greys carrying Mr Walton [presumably the child's grandfather], Miss Walton, the children's aunt, and brothers William and Walter Handford. The second carriage conveyed Messrs Gerard and Hubert Burge and the Misses (2) Burge. Many others were in attendance including Mr J M Phillpotts, Headmaster of the Grammar School. Mrs Farrar's brougham transported the lady and her two sons, and at the cemetery the procession was joined by Dr Prior, the family's medical attendant, Dr Steinmetz, the Rev. W E Bolland and Mr Dymock, Masters at the Grammar School, and Colonels Cross and Macadam.

Eight fellow pupils from the Grammar School carried the coffin with dignity, by means of white tassels, four pupils each side; the violet pall fringed with white silk covered the coffin which was spread with colourful wreaths of flowers in moving tribute from grieving family and friends. The young pall-bearers, named as Masters Kennedy and Prior, Sergeant and Hatchell, Piper and Hill, McNiel and Cockburn, placed a number of floral crosses on the coffin.

The Grammar School 1877

John's grave is not far from the entrance to the cemetery and close to the Bedford Park. It is sheltered by a beautiful shimmering red copper beech tree. The white marble memorial, flecked with black, is maintained and regularly cleaned by The Friends of Foster Hill Road Cemetery.

Author's Note:

The Handford family were representative of the large proportion of Bedford residents associated with India and the Colonies in the 19th century. It is believed that the majority of these families were attracted to the town owing to the fine reputation of the many educational establishments and the Harpur endowments.

John Fraser Handford's brother William Boycott Handford born 5 November 1862 attended the Grammar School 1872-1881 and Walter Walton Handford born 21 April 1864 attended 1872-1883. Both boys were athletic 'as well as being scholars', with William going on to Christ's College, Cambridge on a scholarship and Walter to Trinity College, Cambridge; he graduated at Trinity and after serving curacies at St Giles's, Cripplegate, and East Grinstead, became Vicar in 1906. He died of pneumonia at East Grinstead on 18th January 1918. (Morning Post). It appears that Walter had two sons, Claude and Basil.

William eventually returned to India and in January 1902 a notice appeared in the *Bedfordshire Mercury* announcing that 'The Rev. William Boycott Handford MA, chaplain of Peshawar, was appointed to Dalhousie, Punjab, India.' He married Margaret Emma Peard of Edgecombe, Croydon, on 28 August 1890, with his brother Walter assisting the Rev. R.W. Hoire, Vicar of St Michael and All Angels, Croydon. After a lengthy career in

England and India, William returned to England in 1911 and served in the Great War and World War II.

John's sister Janie E Handford was married at St Paul's Church, Bedford in July 1899 to Mr Wrey and the Bedfordshire Times and Independent reported on 14 July 1899 as follows:

'On Wednesday afternoon a fashionable wedding took place at St Paul's Church when Miss Janie Handford of 14 St Michael's road, was married to Mr Wrey. An extraordinary number of carriages brought the guests to the Church, and after the ceremony, about 350 were entertained in Mrs. Shaw's ball-room, St. Cuthbert's street, which was handsomely decorated and upholstered. Miss Handford was secretary to the High School Guild, who presented her with a silver Queen Anne tray and other gifts. The bridegroom's presents to the bride were, a diamond and ruby ring, Indian silver bangles with mounted tiger claws, Indian silver bowl, modele de luxe bicycle, silver and gold dress embroideries, Indian sunshade, and Encyclopaedia Britannica on revolving stand. The other presents were numerous and valuable. The newly-wedded couple are going to India. When they started for the station, they were pelted with rose-leaves, confetti, rice, and satin slippers, of which one was fastened to the coachman's whip, another to the pole, and a third in the top of the carriage.'

The marriage of Janie to her 'Mr Wrey' was shortlived since the 1911 census reveals that Janie E Wrey was widowed, aged 43 and head of the family. She was living with her mother and aunt Amy, who was still single. As for John's sister Amy Elizabeth

Handford, she married Claude Herbert on 10th November 1895 at Bedford. Her husband was an Indian Army Major. Their only son, Claude Handford Herbert, was born on 16th September 1896 at Dharmsala. Their daughter Doris Geraldine was born four years later. Their son Claude died on 11th November 1918; he is buried in the Staglieno Cemetery in Genoa.

Amy and her husband returned to England sometime between 1918 and 1922 when their daughter, Doris Geraldine, married on 6th September at St Paul's Church Addlestone, Surrey, where the family had made their home at Holmdale in Church Road. Amy died on 18th March 1943 at St Peter's Memorial Home Woking.

Whatever the achievements of John's siblings, there is no doubt their grief at losing their little brother in such a cruel way would have followed them throughout their lives.

In conclusion, the article on the next page is taken from *The Bedfordshire Times and Independent* 14 July 1939, page 12:

'These two pictures show what has happened to one part of the river in the course of sixty or seventy years. Above is a picture of a boating party on the Ouse well back in the Victorian age. The clothes worn by the people in the picture were the sports attire of that date. The place where the photograph was taken will probably be recognized by no one, and without the information supplied by Mr. Frank Smith, of Oxford, who supplied the print, our photographer would not have been able to supply a comparative picture of the spot – reproduced below – as it is now.

'It is the staunch situated just below Castle Mill, Goldington, whence the party had apparently rowed from Bedford. Another interesting point is revealed by the old picture. In those days the staunch was bridged in order to carry a footpath across, and, to judge by the bystanders on the planks at the time this picture was taken, it was a well-used footpath. It ran between Renhold and Willington, and many people will regret the disappearance of this footpath and, in fact, of all the footpaths crossing the river in that vicinity. The reaches of the Ouse in that direction are unknown to most people.

'One townsman who remembers the staunch as it was in the last century is Mr. John Rogers, of 5 Merton Road, Bedford, who was born at Castle Mill and is one of the family of millers. In those days the river was still used for transport, and the lighters going up to Bedford were a familiar sight at the Mill. Owing to the shallowness of the river at the point where the picture is taken, lock gates were placed a little lower down and these were closed when the lighters wanted to get over the shallows. The effect of the closing of the lock would be to form a little pool below the staunch pictured here, and although the lock-gate has gone now, the river still swells in the form of a pool at this spot today.

'The modern picture shows how much attention has been paid to the staunch in the interval. The bridge and the footpath have gone, and trees surround the spot. Brick walls have been added to strengthen the staunch – and boating parties go there never.'

It is very clear that this part of the river was hazardous at the time the article was written, and was even more so at the time of the Handford family's accident and of John's untimely death.

Sources:

Bedford Parish Registers
1871, 1891 and 1911 Census

The Bedfordshire Times & Independent 14 July 1899/British Newspaper Archive

The Bedfordshire Times & Independent 14 July 1939 and 17 January 1902

Foster Hill Road Cemetery Plan 074

Burial Record grave reference Section E.2203

The Ousel [Bedford Grammar School magazine]

Old Bedfordians Club, Bedford School

OS map (NLS website) lhps://maps.nls.uk Bedfordshire XII.SW pub.1885

Bedford Record Office archives - Castle Mill Goldington

University War List, Crockford

Surrey Mirror 6 September 1890

Photographs:

The Bedford Grammar School, St Paul's Square, Bedford 1877
(Ms Gina Worboys, Old Bedfordians Club, Bedford School)
Boats for hire on the River Ouse before 1900 copyright unknown
(M Nicholson)
Photographs taken 1939 of the Ouse at Cardington Mill
(The Bedfordshire Times and Independent.

THE BODY OF A CHILD FOUND IN THE RIVER

Anonymous

It was a common occurrence for children to drown whilst at play by the River Ouse, which wends its way silently through Bedford, a thriving town during Victoria's reign. Sad as this is and distressing as it no doubt was for their families, what could be sadder than a child deliberately committed to the waters by, one presumes, it's own parents, no matter what the circumstances. The mother who did this, or allowed it to be done, must surely have been desperate, and the following is just one example of disposal by this means:

'An inquest was held at the Swan Inn, Goldington, on Monday afternoon, before Mr. Mark Whyley, county coroner, on the body of a newly born male child, which was found in the river on Saturday afternoon. The following gentlemen were sworn on the jury: Messrs. J. Walker, J. Ell, W. Follett, J. Chapman, T. Grove, W. Bandey, T. Ibbott, E. J. Fossey, J. Skilliter, G. Sutton, R. Marshall, J. Martin, and W. Bennett.

'Emery Smith, carpenter, living in Bedford, was the first witness called. He stated that between three and four o'clock on Saturday afternoon he was fishing in the river near Fenlake, when he saw a parcel caught in the weeds close to the bank. He drew it out with his fishing-rod, and on shifting aside the covering with his foot he saw the face of a child. He called to a boy who was on the other side of the water. He came over and witness suggested that they had better send for Supt. Kennedy. Brockett – the lad he had called – and another boy, named Butterfield, went for the Superintendent, and witness remained until Mr. Kennedy came. A policeman also came with the Superintendent, and he removed the body.

'Edward Wager, carpenter, of New Town, Bedford, said he was fishing in the river on Saturday afternoon about four o'clock, when the last witness, who was fishing in Mr. Gudgeon's field, called his attention to a parcel he had taken out of the river. He went over, and identified it as the same parcel he saw in the river on Sunday week. He saw it from the Embankment; it was then about ten yards on the Bedford side of the summer-house, and was floating down the river.

'In reply to a juryman, witness said he was sure it was the same parcel; he knew it by the wrapper.

'The Coroner: Did you attempt to get it out?

'Witness said he thought it was a dead dog; there was one on the pathway.

'Smith, who was recalled, identified the parcel as the one which was taken from the river.

'James Hare, a labourer in the employ of Mr. Gudgeon, stated that he saw the parcel in the river on Sunday week. It was floating very slowly down the river, but he did not try to get it out. He saw it again on Friday when he was mowing the reeds in a meadow by the side of the river. He touched it with the end of his scythe, and pushed it out of the way. He afterwards saw it on

Saturday when it had been pulled out, and identified it as the parcel he saw before.

'Dr. Prior deposed [to bear witness in court] to having made a post mortem examination of the body. It was enveloped in a piece of dark coloured print or linen, which was tied rather carefully, and pinned. This, however, was very rotten. Underneath was a piece of white linen, which partially enveloped the body. It was that of a full-grown child, being 21 inches in length. He estimated its weight at between 8 and 9 pounds. He had brought weights with him, but he was unable to obtain any scales in the village. Dr. Prior gave a minute description of his examination of the body. It was in an advanced state of decomposition. His conclusion from the state of the intestines was that the child was a healthy one, and that it breathed but very imperfectly.

'A juryman: Do you think it was born alive?

'Dr. Prior said that was a difficult question. It had never breathed perfectly.

'A juryman: Do you consider it was drowned?

'Dr Prior: No, I should not attribute death to drowning.

'The Coroner briefly summed up the evidence. He said the verdict which he thought should be returned was that of "found drowned." the body was enveloped in linen, and if they thought by having it washed they would be able, upon examination, to discover anything which would lead to any clue, they might adjourn.

'Supt. Kennedy suggested that it should be done then, and the linen was washed by P.c. Lansbery in the presence of Dr. Prior.

'The Constable was afterwards examined. He deposed that in

the presence and with the assistance of Supt. Kennedy he had examined the linen, but was unable to find any mark on it which would lead to its identification.

'The jury returned a verdict of "Found Dead."'

This is just another heartbreaking and deplorable case of a child's life being denied at the moment of birth by its own parent, due possibly to circumstances of poverty but more likely to the prejudices prevailing at the time concerning illegitimacy. This cruel practice of disposing of one's own child in the river is unbelievably callous. There is no record of this nameless baby boy other than the inquest report. He may well have been laid to rest in Bedford Cemetery, one of many who died anonymously and was disposed of conveniently.

Rest in peace little boy.

AN ICE FATALITY

Albert Edgar Daniels

Once again a little boy lost whilst out with other children playing by the river. Parents must have been aware of the dangers and warned their children but as we know, young children are adventurous and in the excitement of the moment are distracted and the warnings go unheeded. This is the result.

Hand Court (see over)

It was reported in *The Bedfordshire Times and Independent*, Saturday January 30 1897 that on Tuesday afternoon [presumably 26 January 1897] Mr Mark Whyley (County Coroner) attended at the Swan Inn, Goldington, for the purpose of holding an inquiry into the circumstances surrounding the death of a boy of six years, named Albert Edgar Daniels, of Hand Court, Bedford, son of a marine store dealer.

On 27 January 1897 the Bedford Record published details of the severe weather conditions in particular during the previous week, so severe that it interfered with traffic in the town. It was noted that the local doctor was forced to make his visits in a sleigh! Snowfalls have always attracted children and Bedford River has been frozen over on various occasions, attracting children and adults alike. It appears that little Albert was one such child, captivated by the snowfall and icy conditions he encountered upon leaving school. *The Bedfordshire Times and Independent continues:*

'The unfortunate boy fell into the river at Bedford near the Suspension Bridge on Monday whilst walking on the ice, and the inquest was held at Goldington as that Parish includes a large portion of the Embankment Promenade. The first witness heard was the mother of the boy, who said that at 2 o'clock on Monday she sent him to St Cuthbert's Infants School and he went alone. His brother Edwin, who is a year older, left for the same school a few minutes afterwards. At about five o'clock, Edwin returned and said that his brother was drowned. She did not believe it at first, but other children came to her with the same story, including a little girl named Lenton. The latter said that the boy was about to cross the river on the ice and she asked him to come off but he said he would cross. She then turned away to look at the sweepers on Longholme and when she looked back he was in the water, "bobbing up and down" and trying to clutch the ice. Two boys, the girl said, went to the sweepers on Longholme and called them.'

Skating on the frozen River Ouse c. 1895

At this point Edwin Daniels, Albert's brother, [aged only seven, as noted above] was called into the room and interrogated by the Coroner. He told how they came out of school at four o'clock and went down to the river, with other boys and girls following them. There was some ice on the river and Albert and he went on it, but the other boys did not go on. He, Edwin, had got back to the bank when he saw his brother in the water. Some men came down to the river and he ran home when he could no longer see him.

The newspaper reports that 'John Tyler, a labourer, of Russell-street, Bedford, who was "on guard" on Monday to prevent people from going on to the ice at Longholme, said that he saw the brothers and the other boys go past him to the river. Soon afterwards, one of them ran back and said that there was a little boy in the water. He jumped over the fence and ran to the river where he saw the boy with his chin on the ice at a distance of from seven to eight yards from the bank. Witness shouted "hang on my man, till I fetch the life-buoy" and he ran for the buoy near the Suspension Bridge. He ran back with it and the boys called out that "he was gone". He went to the spot but could see nothing of him. The boy was too far off to be reached without the life-buoy and he (witness) could not swim.

'P.c. Purser spoke to recovering the body which was quite lifeless at ten minutes to six, and Dr. R. H. Coombe, of Bedford, gave the result of an external examination of the body.'

The Jury returned a verdict of "accidentally drowned".

According to some accounts, the children crossed the Suspension Bridge, which would take them close to the boat launching point, and this slipway would have given them easy access onto the frozen river. They made an obvious decision not to go home – and Hand Court was not far from the school – but to go in the opposite direction, leading down to the river. The brothers were so young, and no doubt Edwin must have felt guilty for leading his brother onto the frozen river and into danger. What a sad memory for him to carry throughout his life, being responsible for his little brother's death. Both were of such a tender age and should themselves have been supervised and protected.

The 1891 Census return reveals that the boys' parents were living at 22 Newnham Street and were John Daniels, bottle and metal dealer, and Emily R Daniels, both aged 24. Their two sons are Edwin aged 1 year and Albert 4 months. Ten years later in the 1901 return they are living at 12 Hand Court. Two boys are listed, Edwin Daniels aged 11 and Wallace Daniels aged 6 years and their mother Emily R Daniels aged 33. In the 1911 Census they are living at 25 Newnham Street, and again only Emily, Edwin and Wallace are listed. What then became of John Daniels, the breadwinner, as no occupation is listed for Emily Daniels? With no breadwinner life must have been a struggle.

Newnham Street

The burial record shows that Albert and his brother Edwin John Daniels were living at Hand Court at the time of the drowning. Interesting that the family moved from Newnham Street to Hand Court and then back to Newnham Street some time after losing Albert. It is obvious that they did not have an easy life, and this is borne out by an article in the *Bedfordshire Mercury*, Friday 25 May 1906, which reported that John Daniels of Hand Court was summoned for neglecting his child, Wallace Daniels [aged 11] between January 1 and May 16, in a manner to cause unnecessary suffering.

Wallace was born, it seems, in 1895 and aged about 2 at the time of Albert's drowning.

Inspector Bray asked for a remand of the case until Tuesday's Petty Sessions in custody; prisoner was only arrested after ten o'clock that morning. Prisoner consented, and the case was adjourned till the next day. *Bedford Mercury* 25 May 1906 reveals that he was sentenced to four months imprisonment.

From *The Record,* 26 October 1909: 'John Daniels, Newnham Street, was summoned for using obscene language in Newnham Street, on October 18. He did not appear. P.c. Manning stated that at 10.10 p.m. on October 18 in Newnham Street, defendant, who had had drink, but was not drunk, used disgusting language. Defendant was sent to prison for 14 days without the option of a fine.'

It seems poor Emily and her sons must have found life a struggle but the 1911 Census shows that Edwin aged 21 was working as a Labourer in an 'Electric Engineering Yard' and that Wallace aged 16 was working as an 'Errand Boy' for a grocer.

By this time Emily was 44 and still married; there is no mention of husband John.

The Census return is signed in beautiful handwriting by Emily Rose Daniels. I hope life was getting easier for her by this time, supported by her sons.

Further details of the activities of John Daniels are revealed in *The Bedfordshire Times and Independent*. He was prosecuted for a number of offences such as using obscene language in Mill Street (30.05.1907), in Harper Street for nuisance behaviour (06.09.1907), using obscene language (11.06.1909) and whilst living in Newnham Street, begging (08.12.1911). The 1911 census shows aged 56, that he was in prison. He was involved in receiving stolen goods – copper, zinc, lead – (Saturday 3 March 1894 p.7). John Daniels lived at various addresses 72 Bower Street, 22 Newnham Street, 25 Newnham Street, 12 and 13 Hand Court. He must have set a poor example to his sons, by his irresponsible actions.

Wallace enlisted at the age of 20 and the British Army Records 80 Greyfriars Walk show [enlisting record] that he described himself as a 'window cleaner' aged 20 years 8 months, enlisting on 9 November 1915. His father is named as next-of-kin but the name is struck through and substituted with 'Rose Daniels' [described as 'sister' but believed to be his mother]. His service with the 1st Battalion Bedfordshire Regiment commenced 09.11.1915; between 10.12.16 and 22.05.18 he served in France. It seems John Daniels died on 6 December 1917, presumably whilst Wallace was with his Battalion in France.

What eventually became of Albert's two brothers is for

someone else to investigate. Perhaps they married and had children themselves, happy family lives, and were able to help their mother in her later life.

My story ends here and the only task left to me is to visit the burial place of little Albert; there is no memorial other than the memorial pictured on page 16, inscription below. Poor Albert was not a baby, but was far too young to die and to lose his life in such a cruel way.

IN REMEMBRANCE OF ALL OUR BABIES
SO DEARLY LOVED
"AND HE TOOK THEM UP INTO HIS ARMS
AND BLESSED THEM"

St Mark Chapter 10 Verse 16

Sources:

The Bedfordshire Times and Independent January 30 1897 p.6
The Bedford Mercury, Friday 25 May 1906
Ampthill and District News 30 January 1897
The Bedford Record 27 January 1897 and 26 October 1909

SUDDEN DEATH OF A CHILD

Mary Cottingham

How sad it is to learn that mothers in the 19th century were unable to afford to pay for medical attention for their infant children. Perhaps the child's mother was also embarrassed about the fact that her child was "illegitimate". The use of home remedies could do more harm than good but whatever the circumstances, it is regrettable that such a young life was lost, through poverty, ignorance, fear or embarrassment on the part of her mother.

'An inquiry was held at the Corn Exchange on Saturday afternoon by Dr. Prior, the Borough Coroner, into the circumstances attending the death of Mary Cottingham (the illegitimate child of Mary Hannah Cottingham, a widow, living in River-street), who died on the previous day. The following gentlemen were sworn on the Jury: Messrs. L. Walker (foreman), J. Beatty, George Pratt, Michael Mountayne, A. Smith, T. Robinson, W. Wilkinson, W. Cockerill, F. Source, G. Barnes, J. Tysoe, and W. Gurney. The jury having viewed the body:

'Mrs. Dazley said: I live at 18 River-street. The body which the jury have just seen is that of Mary Cottingham. She was 17 months old and the daughter of Mary Hannah Cottingham. Deceased was born at Cottesbrook, Northamptonshire. Ever since her mother has been living with me the child has been in good health and has always eaten very heartily. She had had a little magnesia once or twice, and the last medicine she received was a little milk of sulphur which her mother said suited her other babies much better. The night before last she went to bed between 7 and 8, and before being put to bed her mother fed her with a little broth. About 7 o'clock in the morning her mother brought her downstairs and dressed her as usual. She said the child had been very poorly, and she had had no rest all night. I thought it was due to her teething; my own baby had been very ill. A little milk of sulphur was given to her soon after eight and the child did not appear to get any the better or any the worse. The mother laid her on the couch in the living-room and I gave it a little corn flour to drink. Her mother afterwards took her upstairs and laid her on the bed. She fetched her down about one and nursed her till three, and again took her upstairs, visiting her two or three times to see how she was. I went up twice between this and four, and I then told her to have medical attendance before we went to bed because I did not like the appearance of the child. She said she would go to Mr. Crick and perhaps he would come and look at it. She said she thought the child was dying, and I, looking at it, said, "I am sure she is." I sent for a woman to come in at once to ask her her opinion of the child, and I went for Mr. Crick, who came in a few minutes. When I got back the child was dead in its mother's arms. The mother had always been kind and affectionate to her. The child had purged and had been sick from 2 o'clock on Thursday. It had no sickness from the time it got up on Friday till 11 o'clock. I did not think the child was dangerously ill, my own child had recently been ill.

I had medical attendance and the mother's reasons for not sending for medical assistance before was on account of the expense.

'In reply to a juryman, witness said the mother had a portion of the broth which she had given her child. She was a cousin of hers, and occasionally went out to work.

'Witness, re-called, gave evidence of the child's illegitimacy. The mother went to keep house for a man whose name she believed was Barratt, and the child was the result.

'Mr. R. H. Coombs, surgeon, stated that he had made a post mortem examination of the body. The appearances were that of a healthy, well-nourished child. There were no marks at all on the body. In his opinion death was occasioned by the vomiting and diarrhoea. He did not think it was prudent to give the child milk of sulphur. It appeared to have been a very severe attack; a doctor might have done something for it. As far as he could make out, the mother seemed to have been attentive to the child. Mr Coombs added that the plea of expense was not valid in Bedford on account of the dispensary.

'The Coroner asked the mother whether she was aware that she could have obtained medical attendance from the Bedford Infirmary on the payment of a small fine?

'Mrs. Cottingham: No sir, I was not.

'In reply to a further question, Mrs Cottingham said the child was not insured in any society.

'The Coroner having summed up, the jury returned a verdict of "Died from natural causes."'

.

Bedford 1831, The Infirmary and Fever Hospital

"The Infirmary was erected, endowed, and supported for the relief of the indigent sick and injured sufferer." It was built in 1803 endowed and supported for the relief of the indigent sick and injured sufferer thanks largely to Samuel Whitbread Esq MP. It was enlarged in 1826 to accommodate 80 patients, surrounded by gravel walks and provided with "chairs". One side of the Infirmary accommodated male patients and the other female. It contained baths and showers. Entry at the rear was through an avenue of trees, together with a "pleasant appearance" when matured. "Most of the nobility and gentry of the county are enrolled among its benefactors." [Matthiason]

Infirmary and Fever Hospital, Bedford, Beds.

Sources:

The Bedfordshire Times and Independent, 23 September 1882, p.6
Burial Record: Age recorded as 1 year 3 months.
Engraving: Welcome Collection (1850) and courtesy of M. Nicholson.
Lithograph after J. Sunman Austin, 1850.
Bedford and Its Environs, J H Matthiason 1831 p.112

SUICIDE OF A BOY IN POTTON

David Crompton

David was a young boy of 14, employed – as was his father – by a local brewer. David worked for the family 'in service' at their home. In 1869 this seems to be a good start in life for a young boy, with regular earnings; what could have driven him to suicide? One wonders if bullying and fear may have caused him distress. How tragic for his life to end in such a way.

'On the 8th instant [a particular moment in time] an inquest was held at the Bird-in-hand, Potton, by M. Whyley, Esq., coroner, on the body of a boy named David Crompton, aged 14, who committed suicide by hanging, under circumstances stated in the following report of the evidence.

'Richard Crompton deposed [to testify or give evidence on oath]: I am the father of the deceased, and work at Mr. Strickland's brewery. On Saturday, the 5th instant, I saw the deceased alive and well. He was employed at Mr. Strickland's since Michaelmas last, to wait at table, clean knives and shoes, &c., and I never heard him make a complaint concerning the place.

'Mary Ann Meeks: I am housemaid at Mr. Strickland's, and have been in that situation for three years. I last saw the deceased about 25 minutes past six on Saturday evening at Mr.

Strickland's. He was taking a teapot to the dining room. I had no dispute with him on the Saturday. We had words on some occasions about a handkerchief of mine, but this was only play. I never scolded him or found fault with him on the Saturday. I never heard him threaten to do what he has done, nor did I hear that he had a dispute with any one on Saturday. He generally attended to his work, but was rather a passionate [characterized by intense emotion] boy. We have had no words for a month. I went to look for the deceased about ten minutes after 5 o'clock, and found him in the loft. He was hanging from the beam by a piece of rope around his neck. I called for aid and Charles Head came up. I then went to tell Miss Dickerson who lives at the house.

'Charles Head: I work at the brewery, and on Saturday evening, in consequence of the alarm, I went to the loft and saw the deceased hanging by the neck from a beam, his feet not quite touching the ground. I cut him down directly and sent for a doctor. Having obtained assistance, we had the body removed into the yard.

'Mary Ann Meeks (recalled): The deceased was in the kitchen with me about 4 o'clock on the Saturday. He was wiping the dishes after I had washed them, and broke one dish belonging to the dinner service. He seemed much distressed. He said "What shall I do? I said "It can't be helped." He then said "I shan't tell Miss Dickerson; I shall leave it till Miss Strickland comes home." He then went to his work.

'Mr Henry Raynes, surgeon, deposed that he examined the body, and that deceased had been suffocated by strangling.

'The Jury returned a verdict in accordance with this evidence, that the deceased had died from suffocation.'

Potton was a town of less than 2,000 people at this time, situated about 11.5 miles from Bedford. Straw plait was the principle manufacture. Thomas Strickland, maltster and brewer resided in Sun Street.

No doubt this young boy felt overwhelmed by the responsibility of his position in the middle-class household, and criticism from other members of staff could serve to lower his self-esteem. He was possibly in fear of dismissal. It is a very sorry story and a great pity that such anxiety ended his young life.

Sources:

The Bedfordshire Times & Bedfordshire Independent, Tuesday June 15 1869, p.8
Potton History Soc (Trade Directories) 1867, Potton
The Post Office Directory

INQUEST ON A CHILD

Baby Bromwell

Unless declared to be 'still-born' by a midwife or doctor, a child born unattended but then dying must raise doubts concerning its demise. Here we have a typical case, particularly as it was 'illegitimate' and likely to be an unaffordable burden on its unfortunate mother.

'An inquest was held on Friday afternoon [c. 11 July 1891] at the New Inn, Tavistock Street, Bedford, before Dr Prior, on the body of the illegitimate child of Louisa Bromwell, of Tavistock Place. A jury of fourteen members was sworn in, with Mr E. Rabbitt as Foreman. Following the jury's viewing of the child's body the following evidence was produced.

'Mrs Emily Clarke of 3 Tavistock Place, St Paul's, Bedford deposed [witnessed in court] that the body just viewed by the jury was the child of Louisa Bromwell, a dressmaker. Witness was called in to her neighbour's house very early on Thursday morning where she found the girl in great pain, but denying any serious condition. Medicine was sent for but a child was born a few hours afterwards, when Louisa cried 'Oh, what shall I do' and ran out into the yard. No one was in the front room when the child was born, as Mrs Bromwell had gone to a neighbour's house to get assistance.

'Mrs Rebecca Bromwell said that she was the mother of Louisa Bromwell, who was 22 this month. She had frequently questioned her daughter during the last three months, but she always denied her condition.

'Dr. Mandel stated that Louisa Bromwell had been for some time a patient of his, though he had not seen her recently. She suffered from anaemia. He was called to the house on Thursday morning, and found the body, that of a full-grown male child. There was a bruise on the right frontal bone, the nose flattened, and the mouth firmly closed. There was no disease and he found on a post mortem examination that the child had evidently been born alive. Death had been caused by asphyxia, after the fall at the birth.

'Mrs Monk also gave evidence.

'The Coroner, in summing up, said that the jury should rather seriously and carefully look into such a case as this, because the number of illegitimate children that died in the first year was something enormous. It was very proper that an inquest should be held in such a case.

'The jury, after short consideration, found a verdict of "Accidental death", but thought that there was neglect on the part of the girl for concealing her state.'

The child was born c. 3 July 1891 and was buried 4 July 1891. The recorded age was one day. There is no memorial and there are earlier burials in this grave. Thomas Gentle aged 59 was buried 15 May 1891 and the address recorded as Tavistock Place, Bedford. Richard Marshall was buried 5 January 1946 aged 85, of Rothsay Place, Bedford.

Louisa was obviously terrified of the shame and condemnation of having a child out of wedlock, and no doubt unable to support a child in her circumstances. How sad that the little boy's life was sacrificed – another life lost to the already 'enormous' number of illegitimate child deaths.

Louisa's parents were Joseph and Rebecca Bromwell, coal porter and charwoman aged 43 and 44 respectively. Listed in the 1891 census is Harry aged 25, brickmaker [or possibly bookmaker], Louisa aged 20, and living at 4 Tavistock Place.

Poor little boy to lose his life immediately after birth and to be buried the following day in a three-persons unmarked grave. Unwanted children were easily disposed of.

Source:

The Bedfordshire Mercury, Saturday July 11 1891

GAMBLINGAY MANSLAUGHTER

Nellie Barford

Both parents in this case, were responsible for the death of their little daughter Nellie, only ten months old, as is apparent here.

'The adjourned inquest on the body of Nellie Barford, aged ten months, was held on Monday evening last, at the Heath before the Deputy Coroner Mr. J. Bonnett. Further evidence was brought forward, and the first witness was Mr. S. Burgess, assistant to Dr. Walker, of Potton, who stated that he had attended John Barford, the father of the child, and on the 19th February and the week previous to that date, he had seen him downstairs, for he was then convalescent, and at no time stated that, by ticket from the Rev. J. Watkins, he had sent to John Barford on five occasions, one shillingsworth of meat, once in January and four times in February. William Webb, a gardener at Woodbury Hall said that on several occasions by order of Mrs Astell, he had taken soup for John Barford, and had also given him one shilling from the Baptist Sick Fund. Emma Petch, assistant dairy-maid at the Woodbury Hall Farm, said that by order of Mrs. Astell, she had sent to John Barford during the months of January and February, twice a week from two to three pints of milk, free of any charge. Evidence was also given to say that the man had received regularly his sick money of 10s (ten shillings) a week, from the club. Evidence adduced [to bring forward] was to show that the parents were not in a destitute condition. Mr. Barford's mother, Phoebe Young, said that she visited her daughter about a month previous to the death of the child and seeing that it looked very ill, told both of the parents that they ought to have a doctor.

'The Coroner, in summing up, explained the difference between murder and manslaughter, and first drew their attention to the fact that it was their duty to find what was the cause of the death of the child and then whether anyone was to blame for that death. He summed up at some length, and quoted several decisions bearing upon the point, and left it to the jury to consider their verdict. In a very short time the jury returned a verdict of manslaughter against John and Lois Barford, the father and mother of the child. The Coroner accordingly made out his warrant, and the father and mother were both committed to take their trial at the next assizes, and witnesses were bound over to appear. John Barford was admitted to bail, and Lois Barford was conveyed to Caxton Police Station, where her husband and herself will shortly be brought before the Magistrates for examination.'

The Case of Child Starvation
Gamblingay

So, how did this case progress?

'John and Lois Barford, of Gamblingay, were brought up before the Caxton Magistrates on the charge of causing the death of their child, Nellie Barford, aged ten months, and both prisoners were committed for trial, the husband being allowed bail.'

Clearly the trial date must have been after March 26 1887 but the Writer could not trace a record of this and of the sentence this couple were given. Most people would agree, I think, that a substantial sentence should have been passed down for the cruelty they inflicted on their infant daughter.

Sources:

The Bedfordshire Standard Saturday March 12, 1887 p.8
The Bedfordshire Standard Saturday March 26, 1887 p.8

CLAPHAM: ACCIDENTALLY KILLED

Sibley Collier

Everyone in Bedford must surely know and have visited the Horse and Groom public house in the village of Clapham near Bedford, an inn of great character and charm, backing onto the river. It is hard to imagine that such a tranquil place had been used for the purpose of holding an inquest but this was usually the case. Inquests were frequently held at the pub local to where the accident or incident occurred.

'On Thursday an inquest was held by Mr. M. Whyley, county coroner, at The Horse and Groom, Clapham, on the body of Sibley Collier, a lad aged 15 years, who met with his death by being wounded on the head by a wheel attached to a "dead anchor" attached to a steam ploughing apparatus.

'Mr. A. Hinton was chosen foreman of the jury.

'Richard Giles, farm manager to Messrs J. and F. Howard, said he lived at the Britannia Farm, Clapham. Deceased had been employed at the farm for about six months and was about 15 years old. On Wednesday morning he was at work as "anchor" boy in a field called The Pastures. His duty was to have steered a travelling anchor which moved on about two or three yards in a parallel line with the fence under the control of the ploughman. [He produced a plan showing how the machinery worked.] The ploughman – James Horrell – told witness that the deceased would do well if he did not get hurt, and witness cautioned the lad. Horrell said the boy was too venturesome. When the plough was returning towards the engine the plough stopped so the witness went to the dead anchor and noticed the wheel had gone from the snatch block. He looked round and saw the wheel on the ground and deceased on his side near it with the oil can under him. He called to the men and Horrell came up directly. He afterwards sent a conveyance for him and drove to Bedford for medical aid. Deceased was at work all day with the travelling anchor on the 4th instant. The time when the accident happened was about 20 minutes to 11. Deceased ought to have been with the travelling anchor and his only duty was to attend to it. The dead anchor was about 250 yards from the travelling anchor. When he first saw the deceased he noticed that the pin and cap of the wheel on the dead anchor were gone and laid on the ground by the deceased. The cap was constructed so that the wheel might be oiled or greased without danger and without the necessity of removing the cap. Deceased had orders not to move from his post. The ploughman had to attend to the dead anchor and he had another man to assist him.

'James Horrell, the ploughman, said he had cautioned the deceased several times as he had not seemed careful. He then corroborated some parts of the evidence of the previous witness.

'James Robinson, a shepherd, said he took the lad home in a cart and he died on the way. He groaned very much but did not speak.

'Dr. C. E. Prior, of Bedford, deposed that he was called to see the deceased whom he found dead in the cart. The injuries to the head were quite sufficient to cause death. These might have been occasioned as described by Mr. Giles.

'The jury returned a verdict that deceased was accidentally killed and that he left his post contrary to express orders.'

Sibley apparently died on 4 November 1878. According to the 1881 census the family comprised his father George, an agricultural labourer, Elizabeth, his mother, a lacemaker, George an agricultural labourer, and Sarah a scholar. Another child was born in 1881. Sibley's death at the age of 15 must have been a cruel blow to his parents, and being informed that he was killed by inadvertently meddling with the wire of a steam plough surely added to their grief. No-one else took responsibility or was named as being negligent in the death of this most unfortunate child.

Source:

The Bedfordshire Times and Independent, Saturday 8 November 1879
Buried at Clapham 8 November 1879, age given as 14.

A BOY DROWNED IN THE RIVER

Albert Bass

Once again our attention centres on the River Ouse, where children have always loved to swim or play in hot weather. Fun times were infrequent for Victorian children and they were accustomed to playing freely out of parental control.

'Mr. Whyley, County Coroner, held an inquest at the King's Arms Inn, on Monday last, relative to the death of Albert Bass, a boy nine years old, who was drowned in the river while bathing, on the previous Saturday.

'Philip Bass, miller, of Cardington, identified the body as that of his son, who, he stated, was working with him in the hay field on Saturday afternoon. About half-past three deceased left the field to go bathing in the river, and half-an-hour later a lad named Trueman, who accompanied him, came running back and informed witness that his son was drowning. Witness at once hastened to the spot and went in the river, but could not find deceased, the water being very muddy. Mr. F. Bartram came up and also went in the water, and succeeded in finding deceased in about ten minutes. There were two deep holes in the river at that spot, but deceased had often bathed there.

'William Trueman, aged seven, stated that he went bathing with deceased, who went in first and suddenly slipped under the water, and witness ran back and told his father.

'Frederick Bartram, water bailiff to the Bedford Angling Club, stated that on hearing what had happened he went into the river to endeavour to find the boy. After diving a few times he dropped down and felt about with his feet, and found deceased stuck fast under a ledge, in about six or seven feet of water. He brought him out and laid him on a straw mattress, which had been procured, and for nearly an hour they tried every means – including hot baths – to restore animation, but without success.

'Dr. Mandel, of Cauldwell-street, Bedford, who was called in at the time of the occurrence, stated that the back was wounded as if it had scraped against something, and the body presented the usual appearances of death by drowning.

'The jury returned a verdict of "Accidental Death."'

So many children have been lost to the river, and the river at Cardington appears to be a particularly dangerous spot. It is surprising that notices were not displayed with warnings, and forbidding swimming. Poor little Albert was only nine; he had been helping his father in the fields possibly on a very hot day, and what child would not be drawn to the river to cool off. Parents must surely have recognised the dangers lurking in an apparent serene and enticing stream. What a pity this father did not forbid his child from entering the water.

The Bailiff was a courageous man whose duties did not include rescues, but he could obviously swim and could have saved the child had the boy not been somehow trapped under a ledge. Unfortunately ten minutes at least underwater meant the boy could not be revived. How terribly sad.

Hulcote (wind and water) Mill was leased to Philip Bass in 1880 and he ran the mill until 1894, but his son, also named Philip took over from 1893. Philip senior died on 4 February 1900. There was a third son, John Bass.

The 1881 census shows the family living at 7 Greenside. Phillip, father, was 27, 'journeyman miller' Cardington, and Elizabeth Bass his wife, aged 32. Also Eleanor aged 4, Albert 2 and Sydney 1. Also living with them was the mother-in-law 74 and 'infirmed'. In 1887 when he died, Albert's age is listed as 9.

Sources:

The Bedfordshire Standard Saturday, July 9, 1887 p.7
The Bedfordshire Mercury 16 February 1900
The Bedfordshire Times & Independent Saturday 9 July 1887 p.8

ALLEGED CHILD MURDER

Isaiah Digby

This article relates to yet another infant death perpetrated, it seems, by the child's own mother. The little boy had reached the age of 15 months when he suffered the trauma which ended his life. What could have induced the mother to murder – if indeed she did – her beautiful and healthy child? Perhaps the local newspaper articles provide the answer.

The Adjourned Inquest

'The inquest on the body of Isaiah Digby, aged fifteen months, whose body was found in the river on Wednesday week, was resumed at the "Swan," Goldington, by Mr. M. Whyley, County Coroner. Mr. H. G. Langley, solicitor, of Bedford, was present. The Coroner read over the evidence taken at the previous sitting, and afterwards Abigail Smith, who had been charged with Mrs. Digby with the murder of the child and afterwards discharged, was called as a witness. She said she was a single woman, living at 34 Tavistock-place, Bedford. She had known Mrs. Digby for about six months; she was a widow. On Saturday, March 19, at 7.30 p.m., she met Mrs. Digby at the "Golden Lion," in River-street. She had the baby with her. At 11 p.m. they both came out and went down Clapham-road, taking the baby. They slept out that night in Clapham Road, by the side of the road. On Sunday morning they both walked to Luton. They started at 7.30 a.m. and had no breakfast, having no money. They got there at 4 p.m., and took lodgings at Mrs. Thorpe's, in Bear-street. They stopped there two nights and a day. Mrs. Digby had the baby with her all the time. They left Luton at 9 a.m. on Tuesday to come to Bedford. They again walked all the way. They had some food before they started. The baby was still with Mrs. Digby. They reached Bedford at 4.30 p.m. and took lodgings at the "Cock," Allhallows-lane. Mrs. Digby had some money and she paid for the beds. They had some food at the "Cock" and went out at about 5 o'clock to the river bridge with the baby. They went back again, and witness left Mrs. Digby near the site of the old police-station in Silver-street. That would be at about seven o'clock. Questioned by the Coroner, witness said she could not tell the time. She reckoned it.   Continuing, witness said she went away to the Kempston-road. When witness left Mrs Digby near the police-station, the latter said that she was going back home to the "Cock." Witness returned to the "Cock" at 9.30 p.m. and found that Mrs. Digby had not come back. Witness went to several places in search of Mrs. Digby and eventually went to the "Cock" but she had not yet arrived. When she went out she met Mrs. Digby coming back. She had, not got the baby with her, and witness asked her where it was. She said "I have left it with a lady at the bottom of the Embankment." Witness said "Perhaps it will be taken better care on but what you're a taking," to which she replied "Perhaps it may."   Witness believed her. They both returned to the "Cock," had some tea and went out again. They went across the old cattle market place and came back again. It wanted two minutes to eleven. They afterwards went to bed. Witness went to sleep but Mrs. Digby seemed very restless and kept waking her. She did not give any answer. As far as she could judge Mrs. Digby did not go to sleep at all. She groaned a little, and kept on saying "Oh dear." She seemed in trouble and distressed. She said "We're here to-night, but I wonder where we shall be a week to-night." Early in the morning she said "I must get up, because my inside feels so funny." She got up at half-past six, and left witness in bed. When Mrs. Digby went to bed she was not drunk; she seemed sober. Two policemen came and fetched them away on Wednesday morning, and took them to the borough police-station. Witness had since been set at liberty. On Friday, witness, with her father and mother came to the "Swan," Goldington, and saw the body of the child. It was Mrs. Digby's child. Questioned by Mr. Ell, the Foreman of the Jury, witness said that neither she nor Mrs. Digby mentioned anything about the child on Tuesday night. By another juryman: when they walked to Luton on Sunday, the baby had no food whatever. On Tuesday night witness did not ask her why she was so restless.

'Harry Lawson, Landlord of the "Cock" Inn, All-hallows-lane Bedford, stated that he had known Mrs. Chapman, otherwise Mrs. Digby, for the last fourteen months. She lodged at his house on Tuesday night. She was also there on Saturday with her child. On Tuesday night when she came to pay for the bed she said "You won't charge me to-night for the baby, because I have not got it." He said "What have you done with it Mrs. Chapman," to which she replied "I gave it to somebody, I think it will have a good home." Witness replied that he hoped it would. By Mr. Ell: Mrs. Digby did not seem excited when she was speaking about the baby. She seemed quite sober.

'P.c. Tingey, of the Borough Constabulary, said that on Tuesday, March 22, he was on duty on the Embankment. His attention was attracted to a woman carrying a child. That was at ten minutes to nine. She was going in the direction of Newnham. Witness followed her for about 300 yards. He followed her because he thought she was down there for the purpose of begging. He saw her accost no-one and therefore stopped following. He had no doubt that it was Mrs. Chapman. When he left following she was going towards Newnham.

'Frederick Hills, in the employ of the Corporation, as engine driver at the Irrigation Works, said that on Tuesday, March 22, in the evening, he sent a boy out on an errand. When he thought he ought to be coming back, he went out to look. At a quarter-past nine he saw a woman coming from Bedford towards Goldington. She was carrying a baby. She subsequently went towards Newnham Bridge, from the direction of Goldington. She was shabbily dressed in black. The child had a very light-pink head-gear. He did not take very much notice, as it was not unusual to see a woman there at any time of night, but it was unusual to see one carrying a baby. It would have been a very dark night had it not been for the Irrigation Farm lamps illuminating the roads. Witness lost sight of her then, as she went over the bridge. He was on night duty at the works, and went home at 5.15 a.m. on Wednesday morning. As he was going home he saw a bundle in the river, lodged against a poling [possibly a form of scaffolding] board. He went home and then came back to examine the bundle, but when he got there he found that it had been taken out. He saw Chandler there, who told him that it was a child and that he was going to inform the police. He recognised the pink head-gear he had seen on the child the woman was carrying. Later on in the morning he went to Bedford to the County Police Station to tell them that there might be a woman in the river, as he had seen one walking about there. He saw P.c. Purser who asked him if he could identify the woman. He went to the Borough Police Station, where they took him into a private room. They then took him into the yard, where he saw five or six women. He was asked to pick the one he had seen the previous night and he did so. Her name was Digby. When he picked the woman Digby out she looked at him rather suspiciously, but she did not say anything.

'Jane Pickering was re-called, and said that it was at ten o'clock that she asked Digby where her child was, to which she replied "What's that to do with you. It's all right."

'Abigail Smith, recalled, said that when she and Mrs. Digby went out at 5 p.m. with the baby and returned without it, they left it with Bullet-eyed Jenny Birch at the "Black Swan." She added that she could not write or read.

'The Coroner said that that was all the evidence that would be brought before them, and he would like to know whether it was sufficient, or whether they wanted to know anything more. The Foreman said that the Jury would like to discuss the matter amongst themselves, and all persons besides jurymen were requested to leave. At the expiration of about an hour, the Press were called in, and the Coroner stated that the Jury were not satisfied with the evidence, and they wished to know something further. They had made a request to him to have the body disinterred and a post-mortem examination made. He would therefore adjourn the inquiry until Thursday, April 7.

'We understand that the point at issue is whether the child was dead before being thrown in the river, and it is expected that the post-mortem examination will prove this one way or the other. The Coroner immediately applied to the Home Secretary to have the body disinterred.'

Before the Magistrate

'The woman Digby was brought from Northampton by the 9.45 train on Thursday and appeared before the Magistrates at 11 a.m. The magistrates present were Mr. S. L. Kilpin, Mr. G. Wells and Mr. T. Bull. - Mr. H. G. Langley appeared to prosecute on behalf of the Treasury. - Questioned, the Defendant said that her name was Digby and that she was unmarried. - Mr. Langley asked for a further remand as a post-mortem examination was to be made on the body of the child, and he would like to have the evidence of the doctor. He wanted to give them all the evidence at one sitting instead of piecemeal. - The proceedings were adjourned until Monday.

'We understand that Dr. R. H.Coombs will conduct the post-mortem examination on Friday or Saturday.

Wellingborough Connexions

'A correspondent says that Elizabeth Digby is well-known in Wellingborough and the neighbourhood. She is the widow of a Wellingborough man named Manasseh Chapman. He was the son of a well-known Wellingborough character known by the sobriquet [nickname] of "Doebuck." He was a hawker whose special branch of business was the selling of clothes lines and clothes pegs. He became acquainted with the woman somewhere near Bedford. Some time after the marriage they lived for a short period in Wellingborough, stopping at various lodging-houses. After Chapman's death at Bedford, Digby lived in the White Horse yard. The last time she was seen in Wellingborough was in the month of August last year. She had then her three children with her. She went to the house of a person in St. John's-terrace, and asked permission to stay there for the night. The woman of the house told her that she could not take her, but could make up a bed for the children, and she would have to sit up. She did so, and next morning went out, taking the youngest child with her.

The Alleged Child Murder
Police Court Proceedings
Committed for Trial

'On Monday, the woman Digby, charged with the murder of her son, fifteen months old, by drowning him in the river Ouse on March 22, was brought from Northampton by the 9.45 a.m. train and arrived in Bedford three-quarters of an hour afterwards. She was immediately brought before the magistrates, the Mayor (Mr. George Wells), Mr. T. Bull, and Mr. S. L. Kilpin, and charged with the murder of her child. During the whole course of the proceedings, the defendant looked unconcerned, as if she did not understand the nature of the charge against her. She was accompanied in the dock by a female attendant from Northampton Prison.

'Mr. H. G. Langley, of Bedford, prosecuted for the Treasury, and the defendant was defended, out of kindness, by Mr. G. Horn, also of Bedford.

'In opening the case, Mr. Langley said that the charge against the woman was the awful crime of having murdered her own child. Evidence in these cases were generally of a circumstantial nature, but in this particular case there could be no possible doubt that Digby was the guilty person. Mr. Langley then briefly recapitulated the evidence which he was going to call. He made particular reference to the evidence of a woman named Titmus, who on Tuesday was asked by Digby to hold the child whilst she went out. On returning, the child was handed back, whereupon Digby said "Oh I wish you would keep it for always." This was from a mother to a comparative stranger. He also called the attention of the magistrates to the different excuses given by Digby as to what she had done with the child. Mr Langley concluded by saying that there was a prima facie case upon which to send the woman to trial upon this charge.

'Mr. Horn said that he was going to defend, but did not intend cross-examining the witness, as the case was bound to go to trial and he would rather reserve the defence.

'A greater part of the evidence brought forward on Monday was given at the inquest on the body of the child and we propose giving only a brief resume of that evidence.

'William Edward Chandler, employed by the Corporation at the Newnham baths, proved the finding of the body, on Wednesday morning, March 23, in the river.

'Abigail Smith, who had at first been charged with Mrs. Digby with the murder of the child and afterwards discharged, was the next witness. She said that on Saturday, March 19, she and Mrs. Digby walked to Luton and returned on the following Tuesday. They took lodgings at the "Cock," Allhallows-lane. They went out and left the baby with Mrs. Titmus at the "Black Swan." They returned to the "Cock" and had tea. They again went out as far as the water bridge in High-street, and after some time returned and witness left Mrs. Digby at the site of the old police station. It was at 10 p.m. when she again saw Mrs. Digby and she asked her where she had been. Mrs. Digby said "If you had been looking for me, you would have found me, as I have only been up the street." Witness then asked her where the baby was, and to that Mrs. Digby replied "I have left it with a lady at the bottom of the embankment." An hour later they went to bed, but the defendant did not sleep well. She had a very bad night.

'Jane Titmus, of 29 Allhallows-lane, said that on Tuesday, March 22, between six and seven, she was at the "Black Swan." She saw the defendant with the baby, and Mrs. Digby asked her to hold it. Witness did so, and on the return of Mrs. Digby she told her that she was tired of holding it. Mrs. Digby said "I wish you would keep my baby for always." Witness told her that she could not on account of her illness. Witness said that she had known Mrs. Digby and that she was always kind to her children before.

'Jane Pickering, a servant employed at the "Cock" Inn, said that on Tuesday evening, when the defendant was having supper, she asked her where the baby was. Mrs. Digby replied, "What is that to do with you? It is all right." Witness said, "Isn't the baby going to sleep with you tonight" and she said "No." Witness went on "Won't you take it with you to Northampton tomorrow?" She replied "No". Witness then asked her if she would have it again and Mrs. Digby replied "I don't think so."

Harry Lawson, landlord of the "Cock" Inn, Allhallows-lane, said that he had known the defendant for about fourteen months. On Tuesday night she came to pay for her lodgings. She said "you won't charge me for the baby tonight, because I have not got it." He said "What have you done with it Mrs. Chapman," to which she replied "I give it to somebody, I think it will have a good home." Witness added that he hoped it would.

'Edward Chandler, a labourer of 12 Russell-street, said that he knew the defendant. On Tuesday, March 22 at 10.30 p.m. he was in the "Golden Lion," Midland-road, when Mrs. Digby came to the door and called him out. Witness asked her where the baby was, but she gave no answer. He asked her again and she replied "That's all right, I have put it aside for a time."

'Mrs. Mead, a midwife, of 7, Commercial-road, Bedford, said that in December 1896, she nursed the defendant when she was confined. On Tuesday March 22, she saw the defendant, who came to her house with the baby. She said that she had just walked from Luton and was very tired. She said that she had no money to pay for her lodgings and witness gave her a few coppers. That was between five and six o'clock. The child, when she saw it on the Tuesday, looked like a neglected child.

'P.c. Tingey, of the Borough Police, said that on Tuesday, March 22, he was on duty on the embankment. He noticed a woman carrying a child. It was Mrs. Chapman, the defendant. She was going towards Newnham. Witness followed her and stopped doing so when she was opposite Rothsay-road.

'Abigail Tripp, a widow of 52, Castle-hill, said that on Tuesday evening, March 22, she was down the embankment, walking towards the Suspension Bridge. She noticed a woman carrying a bundle, looking into the water. The woman she saw was Mrs. Digby.

'Bertha Stevens, of 25, Newnham-street, who accompanied the last witness, corroborated her evidence.

'Frederick Hills, of Newnham Cottage, near Bedford, employed by the Corporation as engine driver at the Sewage Works, repeated the evidence he gave at the inquest.

'P.c. Purser, of the County Police, said that he conveyed the body to the "Swan," Goldington. He produced the clothing, which he took off the child after the first sitting of the inquest. He caused the body of the child to be buried.

'Josiah Legge, an undertaker, of Harpur-street, said that he received the body from P.c. Purser. He conducted the funeral on Friday, March 25. On Saturday April 2, He again went to Goldington churchyard, when the body was disinterred. He took the body to the Swan," Goldington. He uncrated the coffin, took the body out, and handed it over to Dr. Coombs, and Dr. Phillips.

'Dr. R. H. Coombs, of Bedford said that on Wednesday, March 23, he examined the body. At that time he believed that the child had died from suffocation in the water. On Saturday April 2, he made a post mortem examination of the body. The body was not wasted but was only moderately well nourished. There were no marks of violence, nor fractures of bones. All the internal organs were free from signs of disease. The lungs showed signs of death by drowning. The state of the heart did not actually correspond to the condition usually, but not always, found after death by drowni9ng. He considered that there was an absence of signs which would go to prove that the child died from any other cause than that of suffocation by drowning.

'Dr. F. B. Wilmer Phillips, also of Bedford, said on Saturday he, with Dr. Coombs, conducted a post-mortem examination on the body of the child, Isaiah Digby. His deductions were independent of those of Dr. Coombs. There was no organic disease in any of the organs. The appearances were consistent with death due to suffocation by drowning. There was nothing to indicate death from any other cause. He had heard Dr. Coombs' evidence and quite agreed with the description he gave of the body.

'Inspector Setchell said that on Wednesday, March 23, he went to the "Cock" Inn, and in the kitchen he saw the defendant. He asked her to come outside and she did so. He said "The body of a child, strongly resembling yours, has been found in the river this morning. I am going to ask you some questions. Before doing so I caution you that you are not obliged to say anything in answer unless you wish to." The following conversation then took place:

Witness: Where is your child you had last night?

Prisoner: My child is in London with my sister.

Witness: Where does your sister live?

Prisoner: I don't know; she is married to John Smith, a mush-faker (umbrella repairer)

Witness: where were they when you gave them the child?

Prisoner: I saw them both in Midland-road near Mr. Cameron's shop, about a quarter to eight last night. The husband said he would keep the child and had a good part by it, so I let him have it and have not seen it since.

'Witness then took her to the Police Station whilst he made enquiries as to her statement and subsequently he charged her with the murder, and in answer she said "I have got nothing to say, except what I have said."

'The prisoner was then charged and on the advice of her solicitor, said she had nothing to say and wished to reserve her defence.

'The Bench then committed her to take her trial at the Assizes.'

The Alleged Child Murder
Verdict of Wilful Murder

'The adjourned inquest on the body of Isaiah Digby aged about fifteen months, which was found in the river near the Newnham Baths, was resumed by Mr. Mark Whyley (County Coroner), at the "Swan" Inn, Goldington, on Tuesday afternoon. The first witness called was:

'Dr. R. H. Coombs, of Bedford, who said that on April 2 he made a post mortem examination of the body of Isaiah Digby. The body was emaciated but could only be described as moderately well nourished. There were no marks of violence and no fractures of any bones. All the internal organs were free from signs of disease. The lungs showed signs of death by drowning. The state of the heart did not actually correspond with the condition, usually, but not always, found after death by drowning. There was absence of signs which go to prove that the child died from any other cause than that of suffocation.

'Dr. F. B. Willmer Phillips, also of Bedford, said that he assisted Dr. Coombs in making the post mortem examination. There was no sign of disease in the brain, lungs, heart, liver or kidneys. The appearances exhibited by he lungs were those due to death by drowning.

'Dr. Thomas Stevenson, Scientific Analyst to the Home Office and Public Analyst for Bedford, said that on April 6 he received a sealed jar containing the stomach, heart, and lungs of a child. There were no appearances of disease. He made a minute examination, but no trace of poisonous or noxious substance was discovered.

'Evidence as to the burial in Goldington churchyard was also given.

'The Coroner, in summing up, said that first of all they must dismiss everything which they had heard outside from their minds. It would be idle for him to deny that a woman, named

Digby, had been charged with murder before the Borough Magistrates and had been committed to take her trial, but they must dismiss all thought from their minds. Theirs was a much more important enquiry, which had a more important termination. Their verdict amounted to an indictment, and the case would immediately go to the Petty Jury, their being no necessity for an inquiry before the Grand Jury. Mr. Whyley then went briefly into the evidence of the principal witnesses, and said that Jane Pickering, the servant at the "Cock," had given her evidence in a straight forward manner and it could be believed. With regard to that of Abigail Smith, he was under the impression that she had been, to a certain extent, instructed as to what to remember and what to forget. The impression she gave was that she was, to some extent, a party to the disposal of the child, not that she knew the mother was going to drown it, but she knew that the mother wanted to get rid of it. On getting further into the evidence it was seen that Abigail Smith had nothing to do with the disposal. They had that day had the result of the post mortem examination, supplemented by the report of Dr. Stevenson. The evidence of the medical gentlemen went to show that death was from drowning and there was nothing to indicate death from any other cause. They could take it that the child was not poisoned, and, after the evidence of the medical gentlemen, as certainly true that the deceased was alive when he got or was placed in the water. Without doubt the child belonged to the woman Digby; she was seen going out with it and to come back without it, and she gave confused answers when questioned. If the woman Digby had not been snapped up before they began making their enquiries he would certainly have had her there, when she would most probably have confessed to being the mother of the child. But she being in custody, it required an order from the Home Secretary for her attendance, and he had not thought it worthwhile to obtain one. It might be said in defence that the woman went out with the child and walked down the embankment, whilst to some extent under the influence of liquor, and that she sat down by the side of the river, and being in a half-drunken state she dropped to sleep. She might have been suddenly awakened and dropped the child, the latter slipping in the river; she might have waded in after it and tried to save it. Against that they must take into consideration that she was not wet and that she did not give that story in answer to questions. It might have occurred accidentally. She might have left the child on the bank, and during her absence it might have rolled into the water, or whilst walking along the river side she stumbled over a reed and let the child fall into the water. Those theories, however, were for another tribunal. If they were satisfied that the child died from drowning, they must either find that it was wilfully drowned, accidentally drowned, or bring in coroner's verdict, that of found drowned. He himself could not come to any other conclusion than that the woman Digby went out with the child, wilfully placed it in the river and drowned it, thereby committing the crime of wilful murder. If that was their opinion it was their duty to say so.

'After a very short retirement the Jury brought in a verdict of "Wilful murder against Elizabeth Ann Digby."'

Unfortunately my story ends here since I could find no details of the sentence Elizabeth Ann Digby was given for such a dreadful crime, difficult to contemplate, of placing one's fifteen-month-old child whilst still alive, in the river to drown on what must have been a very cold March evening. She had three children and we do not know what became of the two she apparently abandoned. She had no home, no means of support and an infant child to care for and must have been desperate. She could have sought shelter in a Workhouse which would have been a place of safety and support, however meagre. Only she would know why she did not choose this option. She must have been distressed, as anyone would in such circumstances.

Although this account is lengthy, it is detailed and gives a clear picture of the events leading up to little Isaiah's tragic death. It is as recorded by the local Press on the following dates.

Sources:

Bedfordshire Times and Independent, Friday April 1, 1898 p.7
Bedfordshire Times and Independent, Friday April 8, 1898 p.6
Bedfordshire Times and Independent, Friday April 15, 1898 p.6
Bedfordshire Times and Independent, Friday April 29 1898 p.7

DEATH AT BEDFORD INFIRMARY

Henry Ekins

'On the afternoon of Wednesday, the 4th inst., Dr. Prior, Borough Coroner held an inquest at the above institution to inquire into the cause of death of Henry Ekins, a boy 12 years of age, the son of a shoemaker living at Risely. It appeared that deceased had been admitted as an in-patient about ten days previously suffering from inflammation of the brain, of which disease he died on the 2nd inst. A rumour having gained circulation that the boy's illness was the result of ill treatment on the part of a woman named Piercy Law, acting in the capacity of house-keeper to the deceased's father, the Coroner in his address to the jury impressed upon them the necessity of weighing well the evidence that would be brought before them, as the case might possibly resolve itself into a charge of manslaughter against the woman alluded to.

'The jury retired to view the body, and on their return the following witnesses were called: Sarah Rootham, a lace-maker at Risely deposed [to bear witness in court] as follows: I am a widow, and live next door to deceased's father, Peter Ekins, who is a shoemaker, and who informed witness that about a year and a half ago, Piercy Law, his housekeeper, had hit the boy on the head with a brush. Witness did not see the blow struck herself, but heard the boy at the time cry out "My head, my head," and although the boy had never been what might be called a healthy child, he complained of his head ever after. Witness had heard Piercy Law often ill-treat and abuse both the deceased and the younger children, and on remonstrating with her on the cruelty of her conduct she said it was no business of hers. Although witness's husband was brother to the deceased's mother, she never went into the house, as Piercy Law was always so uncivil to her, and seemed to be jealous of her wanting the place herself.

'In answer to Mr. Johnson, house surgeon, witness said that during the time the boy's father was in the Infirmary last winter, she could not say that Piercy otherwise ill-used the boy than giving him insufficient food, and subjecting him to cold, there being little or no fire in the place.

'Peter Ekins, the father of the boy sworn: The deceased is my son. Piercy Law was my house-keeper, my wife having died about two years ago. I never saw Piercy Law ill-treat the children when I was at home. About a year and a half ago I was told by a man who worked with me that she had struck deceased on the head with a brush. I made no examination of the boy's head at the time, supposing that he was hurt, as he continued on much the same as he had done before until within about the last three months, when he complained of his head. The boy had always been well treated when I was at home, but differently I have been told when I was absent. During my stay in the Infirmary in the months of November and December last I had been told that Piercy Law had treated the deceased very ill by not giving him proper food, such as he always had when I was at home. I had heard that she had given him sop bread [bread soaked in a liquid eg milk] for his supper when he came home from work.

'By the Coroner: Finding that my son got worse within the last three months, and was obliged to give up work for a fortnight last Saturday, I got a paper to admit him to the Infirmary.

'The foreman of the jury having asked the witness what means Piercy Law had for the support of the three children, during the time he himself was in the Infirmary, he stated that she had 10s [ten shillings] a week from the club, 2s. 6d. weekly that deceased earned, besides four loaves from the parish. When he was informed of her cruelty to the children he reproved her for doing so; she admitted doing it and promised not to do so again. The reason he continued to keep Piercy Law in his service was that he did not know where to look for another house-keeper. He gave her sixpence a week and her victuals [food or provisions] for keeping his house and looking after his children; besides which she had opportunities of making something by her lace pillow.

'Elizabeth Smith, a sick nurse at the Infirmary, sworn: Deceased was brought here a week last Saturday, suffering from violent pain in the head. He was sensible when he was received but became at times insensible. On Monday night, two days after his admission, being at the time quite sensible, he told me how ill the housekeeper had behaved to him. On my asking him where he felt the pain he put up his hand to his forehead as the place he was suffering from. He told me the housekeeper hit him in the head with a brush a long time ago, and that John Ingoldsby (since dead) a person who worked with his father, was standing on the stairs at the time and saw her do it. He also told me that he had suffered from the effects of that blow ever since, and that once when coming home from work he fell down in the field through giddiness. The reason he gave me for the housekeeper's striking him on that occasion was, that when he returned from his work she asked him to fetch in some coals, when he said he felt so giddy he could not do it; and that she (the housekeeper) then said to him - "Oh, you devil, I wish you was dead." Deceased also informed me that Piercy Law was in the habit of ill-using the two younger children, which made him fret very much.

'William Greaves Johnson, house surgeon of the institution, sworn: Deceased was brought to the Infirmary on the 23rd of April, suffering from acute inflammation of the brain, but not in an active form; he had constant pain in the head, occasional sickness, and was generally moaning. On the Tuesday morning, after making the statement given by the nurse, I asked deceased where he felt the pain. He was unable to speak then, but pointed to his forehead. Other symptoms of inflammation followed in succession, namely, squinting, dropping the eyelid, and finally insensibility. Death took place about six o'clock on Monday evening, the 2nd inst. I made a post mortem examination of the body, and found the membranes of the brain highly vascular, the large veins being filled with blood; the ventricles were distended with fluid, and at the base of the brain there was a patch of yellow adhesive lymph; there was also some softening of portions of the brain and one of the ventrical arteries was plugged with fibrine [a white insoluble elastic protein formed from fibrinogen when blood clots]. There was no fracture. I am of opinion that death was occasioned by inflammation of the brain. Having heard the evidence of former witnesses, I incline to the opinion, from the state of the brain, that what I have described might have been caused by a blow at some distant time. The witness, in confirmation of the opinion he had thus formed, then proceeded to site from the work of Dr. Erickson, a high medical authority, wherein it was laid down, in cases similar to that now under consideration, that death might ensue from injuries received a year or two after they had been inflicted; but that mental emotion or any exciting causes might accelerate death more suddenly.

'In answer to questions by the jury, the witness said he was not prepared to say that death in the present case was the result of the blow referred to a year and a half ago; there were many predisposing causes to different diseases which he in[n]umerated; and he must admit that there was nothing in the condition of the brain but what might have been occasioned by natural causes, injury to the brain, in whatever way it might have originated, rendering the patient liable to dangerous illness on the slightest exciting cause.

'The Coroner, in his observations upon the case, stated to the jury that they might very probably, from the medical evidence adduced [brought forward], feel convinced that death in the present instance was traceable to the blow given by the brush a year and a half ago, even then it was necessary in law that it should have been inflicted within the year in order to bring in a verdict of manslaughter against Piercy Law. There could be no moral doubt that that woman had illused the children under her charge, and was therefore highly culpable; but they must be fully satisfied that death was clearly connected with the injuries inflicted within the period before they could send the woman for trial.

'The jury, after a brief deliberation brought in the following verdict; - "That the boy died from inflammation of the brain, but how that inflammation originated there was not sufficient evidence before them to determine."

'After the delivery of the verdict the father of the deceased was called in and remonstrated with upon the fact of his continuing to have such a woman about his premises such as Piercy Law, who was known to illuse his children, when he promised that he would have no more to do with her.

'The housekeeper was also called in and seriously addressed by the coroner on the very narrow escape she had made from being sent to trial. He would therefore admonish her to be more merciful in her treatment for the future.'

I am sure that many readers would feel as I do, that the punishment did not fit the crime. Henry and the other children deserved better and my heart goes out to them. This child lost his life at the age of 12; he was working and helping to support the family and yet subjected to such cruel treatment.

Source:

The Bedford Times and Bedfordshire Independent, May 10, 1870 p.8

DEATH OF A CHILD FROM BURNS

Frederick George Garner

It was reported in *The Bedfordshire Mercury* on Saturday April 5 1890 that an Inquest was held at the Bedford Infirmary on Friday March 29 before Dr Price, Coroner regarding the death of Frederick George Garner, age seven, who died from injuries received from being burned on the previous Wednesday [March 27 1890]. Mr Wright was foreman of the Jury and the following evidence was given.

'Geo Wm Garner said: "I am a carter residing in Pilcroft street [No 29]. The body which has been shown to the jury is that of my son. He was seven years old".

'Mercy Garner said: "I am the wife of the last witness, and mother of the deceased. About a quarter past 7 am on Wednesday last I was in my bedroom. The child got out of bed and ran downstairs from his own room. Almost immediately afterwards I heard him speak to his brother. In Two minutes after he said "mother my nightshirt is all on fire". I rushed down and he met me at the stairs door, his shirt all in a blaze. He had been very poorly and he was in the habit of going downstairs and standing before the fire to dress. I pulled the shirt off as quickly as possible. He had a tight fitting vest underneath, which was difficult to get off, but my hands were much burnt in doing so.

Then I got hold of a cloth and wrapped it around him, and I ran to Mrs Burnham, my neighbour. When I got back he said "let me go to bed mother" and he ran upstairs and got into bed. He was not at play with the fire. We have a fire guard, but it is not put up till the children are dressed. He had a foot on the fender, and was looking out of the window at the time.'

'Mrs Burnham said: "I reside next door to the last witness. I was called by her on Wednesday morning at 7.30. I heard her say that her boy was burnt. I ran immediately and found him in bed covered up with sheets. I could see that he was badly burned in most parts of his body. I got some flour and sprinkled over him. That seemed to soothe him and he wanted to lay down. My husband went to see for Mr Garner, who went, I believe, to Dr Kinsey, and received directions to bring him to the Infirmary. Dr Kinsey did not come to the house. A fly [a hackney coach] was procured and he was taken to the Infirmary.

'Dr Skelding, house surgeon, said: "The deceased was brought here at 8.14 on Wednesday morning suffering from extensive burns, on the face, hands, chest and abdomen, and it was suffering from the shock. Towards evening he became delirious and died at 9.45 in a fit of convulsions. Death was due to injuries received."

'By a juryman: "About 25 minutes elapsed before I saw the child. I was in bed and I gave directions for the child to be taken upstairs, and two nurses had directions to attend to it, and another nurse attended to the mother. I proceeded to dress and saw the child as soon as I was dressed. The nurses had had considerable experience, and they knew exactly what to do. It might seem a

long time for the father to wait. The burns were quite superficial."
[Surely the above related to Dr Skelding, house surgeon?].

'Another Juryman: "He could not have done any better than the nurses."

'The Coroner said it was an accident which not unfrequently occurred. There was one thing to be noticed: - there was no fireguard, which there ought to have been if children went there to be dressed. The doctor had told them that he was not in a position to see the child when it arrived, but he should say that trained nurses were quite capable of seeing after that. The case did not call for any amount of surgical skill, and he did not see there was the slightest reflection upon Dr Skelding.'

The jury returned a verdict of 'Accidental Death'.

'After the verdict had been returned one of the jurymen said he heard that the bandages were taken off by the doctor after the nurses had put them on. If the nurses were capable of doing them what necessity was there for the doctor to take them off again?

'Dr Skelding was then recalled and in answer to the coroner, he said the bandages were not taken off by him, for when he went they had not been applied. It took some time to saturate cotton with oil to put over a whole body. What he did was to lift up the lint just to see if the burns were superficial or deep. The lint covered the whole body, and by lifting it up he found that the burns were superficial. Subsequently the bandages were applied.

'After this explanation the jury said they were satisfied that no reflection could be cast upon Dr Skelding.'

At the time of the accident the family were living at Pilcroft Street, an impoverished area of the town, which was off the Ampthill Road and not far from the Infirmary, which is now the Bedford South Wing Hospital. There appear from the 1891 census to have been three children in the family, Frederick age seven, the eldest, Sidney aged four and Walter aged two. A fourth child, Albert William Garner, died and was buried only two months earlier, on 28 January 1890, aged 11 months. Mention was made of Frederick speaking to his brother once downstairs and that was most likely the four-year-old Sidney, who later said that his brother was standing on the fender and looking out of the window when his night shirt caught fire. Had the fireguard been in place, the accident may not have occurred, so in that respect, the parents were negligent. By the time of the 1891 census the family had moved to 10 Holme Street, prompted perhaps by the tragedy and loss of their two sons.

It would have been common at the time for home remedies to be used to treat illness and this explains the sprinkling of flour over the wounds. Of the many publications advising on and publicising products and home remedies during the Victorian period, there are Household Guides which recommend that burns be covered with flour and wrapped in cotton wadding. In fact, there is still debate online concerning this method of treating burns even today.

There is no doubt that this poor child suffered greatly from the burns he sustained, and perhaps (on reading the script closely) one might suspect that his parents were not entirely satisfied with the treatment he received; for instance, when the incident was reported that morning, no one came to check his wounds and administer assistance, and after a delay in getting to the infirmary, he was not seen by a qualified doctor ('surgeon') but referred to nursing staff to attend to his wounds. There is no mention of pain relief being administered, only that he was 'delirious' - not surprisingly. Dr Skelding mentioned 'extensive burns' and shock; a 'juryman' mentioned that the burns were 'quite superficial' and all in all, it seems, there was little consensus. The poor child was wrapped in bandages and cotton soaked with oil to cover the burns and Dr Skelding stated that he had 'extensive burns'. While the child was being treated by the nurses, it must have seemed a 'very long time' for Frederick's father to wait, until Frederick was seen by a qualified doctor or 'surgeon'. Surely the 'juryman' was not qualified to make a statement that 'the injuries did not require surgical skill'?

It appears from the 1891 census that Dr Robert Kinsey was living at 45 Harpur Street, a fifty-year-old GP born in Lucknow, India. Harpur Street is a fair distance from the boy's home. As the child lay in pain from his burns, the neighbour sent her husband to locate Frederick's father, working as a carter so perhaps not easy to find. Mr Garner had then to visit the doctor at his home in Harpur Street and as directed by Dr Kinsey, went to find transport to convey the child to the Infirmary, and then to rush thelittle boy to the Infirmary and all this, apparently, in the time stated. Notable that the GP did not visit the child at his home to inspect the wounds, but instead directed Mr Garner to take him to The Infirmary. During all this time the child received no medical attention or pain relief, as far as we can tell. There was yet another wait until help was given at the Infirmary – by the nurses (rather than Dr Skelding). In the circumstances it is surprising that poor Frederick did not die sooner; shock must have been a major factor in his demise.

Perhaps it was not only the parents who were guilty of negligence in the care of this child referred to as 'it' on occasions. The 1901 census reveals that Dr Robert H Kinsey, aged 60, was living at 10 Rothsay Gardens and had become Surgeon to HM Prison. He may well have been too busy in his new post to reflect on the misfortunes of children such as Frederick Garner and the sad outcomes.

Pilcroft Street

Little wonder the child had convulsions and died that night. Frederick was buried in Bedford Cemetery on 29 March 1890 [grave 82 D] next to his baby brother Albert, buried 28 January 1890 [grave D6 82]. Sadly there is no headstone or memorial for these precious little ones.

Sleep in peace little Frederick and Albert.

Source:

Bedfordshire Mercury Saturday August 16 1879

MURDER AND SUICIDE AT KEYSOE

Louise Elizabeth Green

It may be that depression or mental illness resulted in infanticide in the late 1800s, but it must surely have been a rare occurrence in a stable middle-class family such as that of a local and well-known miller. Read on.

'This (Thursday) morning an appalling event was found to have occurred at Keysoe, in the family of a highly respectable miller named James Green. It appeared that on Wednesday night he went to bed leaving his wife, Elizabeth Mary Green, downstairs, and that about one o'clock, finding Mrs. Green had not come to bed, he went downstairs, and found her in the living room with her throat cut. The infant daughter, Louise Elizabeth, aged six months, was also found dead in the bassinet, [a wickerwork or wooden cradle] but at the time it was not apparent by what means the child met with its death. Mr. Green immediately sent for assistance, and Mr. P. H. Banks, surgeon, Risely, and P.c. Sturges were soon on the spot. They found that life was extinct in both the bodies, and as the child's upper extremities were very wet, and a tub of water stood outside the door, the theory is that Mrs. Green drowned the child and then committed suicide by cutting her own throat. It is well known that insanity is hereditary in the family on the deceased's side, and there is no question that the mind of the poor woman was deranged at the time she committed the alleged act. An inquest will be held at the Chequers Inn at 10.30 on Saturday morning.'

The Murder and Suicide at Keysoe

'As briefly reported in our last week's issue, a tragic event occurred at Keysoe on Thursday, the 6th inst., when Mr. James Green, miller, found the bodies of his wife and child in his own house, the one having evidently died from a self-inflicted wound in the throat, and the child, as it afterwards transpired, from suffocation by drowning, caused in all probability by the mother while she was suffering from mental derangement. The family is a highly respected one in the neighbourhood, Mr. Green having himself for some time enjoyed the confidence of the parish as overseer and member of the School Board. Mrs. Green also held the esteem of all who knew her, and the unfortunate act by which she met her death can only be attributed to hereditary insanity in the family. As will appear from the depositions at the inquest, members of the deceased's family have either been inmates of asylums or under medical treatment for various degrees of lunacy, and Mrs. Green herself, it would appear, unhappily became a prey to religious mania. The inquest was held at the Chequers Inn, Keysoe, at half-past ten on Saturday morning last, before Mr. Coroner Whyley and the following jury: - Rev. J. Hill Banham (foreman), Messrs. William Brooks, Geo. Walker, James Hartop, John Hartep, B. Hartop, Theo Head, Chas. Roberts, Jno. Wise, Wm Hartop, Jno. Page, Ed. Stapleton, and

Jno. Saunderson. P.s. Cooke, of Riseley, and P.c. Sturgess, of Keysoe, were also present.

'The evidence was as follows: -

'James Green said: I am a miller and live at Keysoe. The deceased, Elizabeth Mary Ann Green, was my wife; she was 37 years of age. Louise Elizabeth Green was my daughter, and she was six months old. I last saw my wife alive about 20 minutes to ten o'clock on Wednesday night. She attended me up to bed and then left me and went downstairs. I left my daughter, Emily, downstairs. She is about 12 years old. I went to sleep and woke up soon after 12 o'clock. My wife had not come back. I felt across the bed several times before I disturbed myself to get up, and finding she had not come I rose. I had no light in the room, but on opening my bedroom door I saw a light in the parlour. I called out several times from the top of the stairs, but received no reply. I went downstairs and looked in at the parlour door. I thought my wife sat asleep in the easy chair; I touched her shoulder and spoke to her. She had her night-dress on, but she was dressed when she left the bedroom. I saw some blood streaming down, but I could not say from where it came. Next I felt for the baby in the cradle, and the body seemed very cold, but I did not notice that it was wet. I was afraid, however that it was dead. I picked up the razor which lay somewhere near, but I am not quite sure whether it was on the floor or the chair. I ran upstairs and awoke my eldest son Francis, 18 years of age, who was at home. We dressed ourselves together, and I went to alarm the neighbours. First I alarmed Freeman, a labourer, whose window contained a light; then I went to Woodward at the Post

Office. They got up and returned with me to our house. I have been married to my present wife 15 years. She has been very desponding [sad, dejected] in her manner, and lately, more so than usual, but she never mentioned that anything in particular was on her mind excepting over religious matters. She sometimes made use of the expression that she was born to be lost. It is not more than three weeks or a month since she manifested despondency on religious subjects. The place of worship which she attended was the Baptist Chapel, but her views were more Calvinistic. [Relating to John Calvin, religious leader]. My wife did not go out on the previous Wednesday, nor had she attended a place of worship for the last two Sundays. She was not more desponding on a Sunday than on any other day. I have never heard her express any intention of destroying herself. Two members of her family, an aunt and a sister, are at present confined in a lunatic asylum; the aunt has been there many years, and the sister about four or five years. The form of their insanity was not religious mania, but her father was subject to it for a year or two before he died. He was not under restraint but he kept his bed, and was not violent. There was nothing unusual in my wife going downstairs to put the child to bed. On the Thursday morning, after looking round the premises, I went to the closet, and there found a pail three parts full of clean water; also a candlestick, candle, and box of matches. The candle had been blown out.

'Thomas Woodward, shoemaker, Keysoe, said: I live in the next house to Mr. Green's. At a little after one on Thursday morning Mr. Green came to my house and called me. I went down and found him in great trouble. I went into the house, took a candle, opened the door, and saw Mrs. Green sitting in a chair. I went up to her, examined her face, and found she was dead. Her nightdress and the room were smothered with blood, and the razor produced was in her right hand. I could see that her throat was cut. In the cot at the side I saw the child; it seemed asleep, and I tried to wake it by taking its hand. There was a little warmth in the body but although I could see no marks, I assured myself that it was dead. Mr. Green sat in the next room, and I went in and told him that they were both dead. He gave way to great distress, and went to awaken the son Francis. I had not seen Mrs. Green for two or three weeks to speak to her, and did not know that she was desponding. To the best of my knowledge Mr. and Mrs. Green lived comfortably together, and the deceased was a particularly good mother and kind to children.

'Mr. T. Banks, surgeon, Risely, said: On Thursday morning last, at a little after one, I was called by Frank Green to come to the Mill to see his mother, who, he said, was bleeding to death. When I got there I saw Mr. Green and some of his neighbours. I arrived a little before two o'clock, and I hurried as much as possible. I saw the deceased, Mrs. Green, in a semi-erect position, sitting in the arm chair, and dead. I looked in the bassinet close by and saw that the child was dead. Then I examined the room to see that there was no disturbance of the furniture to indicate a scuffle, and I found nothing of the kind. Then I went into the room and had a few words with Mr. Green. The body of Mrs. Green I caused to be laid down on the hearthrug; she was dressed in her night dress, with a small black gauze ruffle round the neck. On the head falling back there was a huge gaping wound in the throat. The skin had been cut twice, the razor having evidently been drawn twice across the throat. The trachea, both carotids, the jugular vein, and in fact everything down to the spinal column were cut through, and plainly exposed to view. From the character of the wound there was no doubt that it was self-inflicted, and by such an instrument as the razor produced. I had both hands and arms washed of the blood with which they were saturated, and I found no marks of any kind to indicate a struggle. The right arm was wrapped up in a sheet, but the hand was exposed. Her every-day dress was behind the chair, and I carefully examined this to ascertain if it were wet, but I found it to be quite dry. The night dress, chemise, and under-clothing were saturated with blood. The infant was lying in the bassinet, covered with new flannel of two or three thicknesses, and the body was lying on the same material. The child was quite dead, and the clothes, down to the waist, were wet. I removed them one after the other, and found them wet to the same depth. The eyelids of the child were closed, and the countenance pale; there was no froth, and the skin of the body was natural. I should say that the child had been held in clean water (for there was no stain on the dress) head downwards, and that the infant died from suffocation by drowning. The cause of death of Mrs. Green was loss of blood. I formerly attended her father, who was demented but not violent, and was capable of being treated at home.

'The Coroner said it was not necessary to call Freeman as he would only relate what the jury had heard from Woodward. This was one of the most painful cases it had been his lot to inquire into, but their duty was simple. The facts were so clear that they would have no difficulty in arriving at a proper verdict. The death of Mrs. Green was caused by cutting her throat, and the wound was self-inflicted, and at the time she inflicted that wound she was no doubt of unsound mind. In the case of Louise Elizabeth Green the Jury would have to say that death was caused by suffocation by drowning, and it would also be their duty to say that it was done by the mother. As it was not for them to inquire into her state of mind at the time she committed that act it would be their duty to return a verdict of wilful murder against Mrs. Green. He did not tell them to return these verdicts, but merely indicated them as being consistent with the evidence. The only discrepancy that appeared in the evidence was regard to the position in which the razor was found.

'It was pointed out to the Coroner that there were two razors, the one found by Mr. Green, and the other by Woodward, both of which were produced.

'The Jury acquiesced in the Coroner's view, and returned verdicts in accordance with his directions.

'We may add that the funeral of Mrs. Green and her infant took place on Saturday afternoon at the Keysoe Baptist Chapel, the service being conducted by the pastor, the Rev. Mr. Head, and the inhabitants of the village and neighbourhood showed their sympathy with the bereaved family by attending in large numbers. Mr. Page, of Pertenhall, was the undertaker.'

Many women reading this may wonder why the term 'insanity' was so frequently used, and details of the family history given in some detail. With a child of 6 months of age she may well have been experiencing post-natal depression. When Mr Green called downstairs it is surprising that his older children, one downstairs and others upstairs, did not wake and respond. The information concerning the razor blade(s) was also confusing. It seems to me the jury were easily convinced, and to my mind there remain unanswered questions. Some may agree with me, other not, but I would like to have been there to pose my questions. If Mrs Green was of unsound mind many would say she ought not have been left alone with the unfortunate infant.

Sources:

The Bedfordshire Times and Independent, Saturday, 8th April 1882 p.8
The Bedfordshire Times and Independent, Saturday, 15th April 1882 p.7

ANOTHER LIFE SACRIFICED

Alfred Huber

It was reported in *The Bedfordshire Mercury* on Saturday August 16 1879 [page 7] that 'On Wednesday morning about 9.30, a little fellow named Alfred Huber, 7 years old, son of Mr Huber, cabinet maker, in the employ of Mr F. Hockliffe, furniture dealer, and book seller, St Loyes-street, Bedford, was drowned beside the bridge in the sight of a few young lads who were utterly unable to render help, and, we have reason to believe, in the sight of some adults on the bridge, who were unable to swim, but whose names have not transpired. Two sons of Mr Field, very young boys, were on the steps next the bridge leading down to the water, one of them being fishing, and the deceased happened also to be on the lower step, next the buttress on the left. While here he seems to have stooped over and put his hand in the water, thereby losing his balance, and the next moment he was in the water. He rose three times and then sunk. Shortly afterwards boats were on the spot and dragging was commenced by Inspector Haynes and Mr Goatley (of the boat yard opposite). After about three-quarters of an hour had been spent in dragging, Inspector Haynes succeeded in finding the body at the bottom of the river, in a part where the water is some 12 or 14 feet deep. It was taken to the mortuary as soon as possible, to await the official inquiry.'

The steps and boarding point to the right.

The inquiry was held 'on Thursday last at the Corn Exchange before the Bedford Coroner, Dr C. E. Prior.' A jury of 13 members was sworn in. Inspector Haynes stated that "yesterday morning" between 9 and 10 o'clock he received information from Mr Nash's groom that a lad was in the water at the bridge. He procured the drags from the Police Office at once and proceeded to the spot. He got into a boat and commenced dragging. After dragging about half an hour he hooked the body at the bottom of the river, a few yards beyond the landing place at the steps and in the deep water. There was a moderate current. He conveyed the body to the mortuary.

There were witnesses on the bridge but one 'could not swim and had got gout in the hands and arms.' The Coroner said it was very sad that three cases of drowning should have occurred in rapid succession by the embankment and the bridge, and there was some discussion about the need to fence the area to prevent further accidents but that 'the area by the steps was an ancient water-right of the town'. The jury returned a verdict of Accidental Death.

The newspaper article bears a final comment that 'evidently the value of human life is at a discount just now in Bedford'.

Alfred was buried in Bedford Cemetery on 15 August 1879 [grave section E6 6] and sadly his father Henry Huber died seven months later and was buried on 6 March 1880 aged 32 [grave section E6 16]. Father and son were buried side-by-side. There is no headstone.

Steps down to the Ouse (see also page 219).

As far back as 1868 Bedford Town Council were seriously considering the viability of building a wall by the embankment in order to prevent accidents.

The Bedfordshire Mercury, Saturday May 30 1868 [page 5] carried an article concerning the Bedford Town Council and tenders for completion of the embankment work. 'At the adjourned quarterly meeting of the Town Council held on Wednesday at noon, Mayor T T Gray Esq read the following report of Mr Lawson, the engineer, which was addressed to the board:

'I have examined the four tenders sent in for three different designs, viz:

No 1 ..... Wall having plain brick parapet
No 2 ..... Ditto, terra cotta balusters
No 3 ..... Ditto, Portland stone balusters and pillars'

There followed much detail regarding cost in particular, with design 3 being the most expensive at £2,360 [Winn and Foster, Kempston]. There was a suggestion that the wall was not necessary and that there was no wall at York, Norwich and other places. Alderman Nash proposed that the matter be referred to a committee which would report to the board and this was carried.' Little support was shown for the construction of a wall it has to be said.

The Bedford Times and Bedfordshire Independent, Saturday February 13, 1869 [page 4] carried an article concerning another council meeting in which the river wall was discussed. It states that plans were submitted by Mr Lawson [engineer] regarding the elevation of the proposed embankment and river wall. 'He said it had been suggested that iron columns with tubing or balls should be placed upon the present coping of the river wall, but at times of regattas a great many people would be assembled there, and unless the columns had a very firm foundation there would be a possibility of the structure giving way and precipitating people into the river. From the character of the present work it would not be an easy matter to get the necessary strength in the foundations and therefore he had prepared another design which, though more costly, was more suitable for the wall – brick with stone coping'.

Mr Lawson went on to say that the design is a balustrade somewhat corresponding to that of the bridge and that it would cost about £1 a yard – the whole cost about £250. It was decided to leave the matter until the Board were aware what the Duke intended to do.

On Saturday January 11 1890 [page 5] an article on this subject headed 'The Embankment and the Recent Fatality' appeared in *The Bedfordshire Mercury*. It seems 'The Embankment Committee recommended that the existing stone balustrade be continued to the stone pier opposite Mr Biffen's house. The Committee estimated the cost. Mr Wells said that it was important that a fence of some kind should be put up and the Committee had come to the conclusion that it would be best in many ways to continue the fence that the Duke had put up, and besides, it matched the bridge. Mr Miller said the matter had been considered some years ago and then it was decided that if they did anything it must be in this substantial way, but he was not prepared to say how the payment of it was to be made. He was convinced that they would make a great mistake if they did anything else with it.'

'Dr Paton, the Coroner of the borough said he held an inquest on December 24 last upon the body of a little boy accidentally drowned opposite the Club house, and it was believed there was another body at the present time in the river. At the inquest held at the Kings Arms the jury came to the following resolution: "the jury are of opinion that the present unprotected side of the river along the Embankment is a constant source of danger as shown by several accidents, fatal and non-fatal and they beg earnestly to report to the Town Council that a proper fence is required".' There was yet further discussion about the cost, also about the possibility of children running along a wall and falling into the river. Because of this, an iron fence was deemed to be less dangerous, but that an unclimbable fence would prevent timely assistance in the event of boat accidents.

It was agreed that tenders be obtained for fencing the Embankment in the three different stones previously mentioned by Alderman Young, and also for an iron fence.

Amidst the discussions, objections, costings and concerns, people continued to drown in the river, and although the final outcome, which can be seen to be as safe and secure as possible in addition to being an attractive asset to the town, could not benefit poor little Alfred and others who lost their lives in the river prior to Alfred's death and indeed since.

The Embankment at the time of Alfred's death and present day.

Reference to the 1891 census shows that Alfred's mother Charlotte had a son called Frank some seven years after the death of her husband and aged 4 at the time of the census. Charlotte describes herself as 'Wid' and she was obviously widowed; she uses the surname Huber and there is no husband listed. The children are John 21, Kate 14 and Frank 4, and Charlotte is aged 45. Interesting to note that Charlotte was summoned by J. A. S. Bowden, Vaccination Officer, for neglecting to cause her child to be vaccinated. [*The Bedfordshire Times and Independent 19 May 1888*]. The child was presumably Frank. Also interesting to note that John Huber is later described as 'brother-in-law' in the 1901 census and aged 42. Perhaps this is a second John Huber: the son aged 21 in 1891 emerges as John Huber, Head, 54 and single stone mason in the 1911 census, living with Frank Huber his 'nephew' aged 24; if this is the 4-year old Frank listed in 1891 as 'son' by Charlotte, when Kate was 14 years of age, then he is half brother to John and 17 years his junior!

Just to recap, according to the 1901 census the Huber family are still living at Albert Street and Charlotte is head of the family, 'Wid', 55 and a laundress on 'own account' and working from home. Living with her are Kate 23, a 'cook (domestic)', Frank aged 14, a 'worker' and John Huber 42, 'brother-in-law' and a stone mason. Also listed are Edward Huber 5, and Alfred 2, both described as grandsons. These could be Kate's sons as she is 23 and still using her maiden name. Could they be John Huber's children who is described as brother-in-law by Charlotte? If so, where is John, her son, aged 21 in the 1891 census? After this point life becomes difficult and complicated for poor Kate who was only two at the time of her brother Alfred's death from drowning.

Charlotte Huber died aged 63 in 1909 whilst living at 19 Union Street. It seems she is not buried with her husband Henry. According to the 1911 census the head of the family is George Allen aged 35 and 'single'. He is a house painter. Kate is described as a housekeeper, aged 34 and single. Frederick Huber, son aged 15 is a plumber's (? assistant), Alfred, son aged 12 is at school and Laura Huber aged 8. At this point Kate Huber, still single, has three children. Could George Allen be their

Also in the 1911 census but presumably living at a different address, are:

John Huber, Head, aged 54 and single, and
Frank Huber, nephew, aged 24 and single

John is a stone mason and Frank a mason's labourer.

Finally, in this conundrum one wonders what happened to Edward Huber aged five in 1901 and Charlotte's grandson.

It seems that Charlotte's daughter Kate, and the illegitimate children she bore, had a dreadful life; whoever fathered her children must have been irresponsible and unsupportive, and the marriage she undoubtedly anticipated never transpired. According to *The Bedfordshire Times and Independent*, Friday 9th June 1911 the following occurred:

A Children's Court

There was a Children's Court on Thursday morning, before Mr. G. Royle (in the chair), and Mr J. W. Carter.

Adjourned

Edward Huber, 37 Chandos Street, aged 15, was summoned on a charge of stealing between May 30th and June 1st, a quantity of lead piping, value 7s. 6d., the property of George Haynes. Kate Huber was summoned as parent.

Bedford Borough Police Court
Friday, 21st February 1908. Before Dr. Coombs and Mr. Deane.

A Sad Case

'Kate Huber, of 8 Kerr Street, Northampton, was brought up in custody on a charge of leaving her three children, Frederick, Alfred and Laura Huber, chargeable to the Common Fund of the Bedford Union from the 11th inst. The defendant pleaded guilty.

'Mr. W. Payne, Clerk to the Guardians, appeared to conduct the case on their behalf.

'The Master (Mr. Blimrose) proved the facts that the woman took herself and three children out on Feb. 4, and that the latter were brought back by their grandmother on Feb. 11; the children's ages 12, 9, and 5. The defendant is a cook, and has been in and out of the House for the last three years or more.

'Mr. Payne said the Guardians realised that they would in all probability have to bring the children up, and they were prepared to do so, but they felt the defendant must be shown that she could not go and leave her children in this manner. It was a breach of the Vagrancy Act which the Guardians could not pass over.

'The defendant, in answer to the Bench, said she had hopes of being married and getting a home together for the children.

'The Bench, after careful consideration, adjourned the case for a month, liberating the defendant on her own recognizance of £5 to come up on March 24.'

[Copied from the *Bedfordshire Mercury*, Friday 28th February 1908].

Kate Huber died on 7th March 1923, aged 55 years. She was living at 77 Queens Street Bedford.

[Copied from the *Bedfordshire Times and Independent* 16th March 1923].

It appears that Frederick, Alfred and Laura were abandoned to the Workhouse, but there is still no mention of Edward. Did he continue in his life of criminal activities perhaps? He may have resorted to crime by theft in order to support himself. Little wonder that Kate died so young. Edward was not living with her at the time of her death, when he would have been 30.

In conclusion, and bearing in mind the discussion at Alfred's inquest regarding the potential for accidents at the steps and landing point by Bedford bridge, it wasn't until the 1890s that the balustrade which still stands today was built by the embankment. Iron gates now bar the way to the steps, to prevent unsupervised entry. Perhaps Alfred's death was not in vain and life is no longer 'at a discount in Bedford'.

Sources:

1891, 1901 and 1911 census
Bedfordshire Times and Independent 16 March 1923 and 19 May 1888
Bedfordshire Mercury, Friday 28 February 1908 and 16 August 1879
The Bedfordshire Mercury, Saturday May 30 1868 (p.5)
The Bedford Times & Bedfordshire Independent February 13 1869 (p.4)
The Bedfordshire Mercury, Saturday January 11 1890 (p.5)
Burial records, Bedford Cemetery: grave references E6 16 and E6 6

Photographs:

Views of the bridge and the embankment taken at about the time of the accident, from postcards, origin unknown (M Nicholson)
Present-day views of the steps and the embankment (by the Author)

SAD TALE OF STARVATION

Emma Rebecca Hills

The Bedford Times & Bedfordshire Independent, reported in September 1870 as follows:

'On Monday the 19th inst [instant., moment in time], an inquest was held in the Board-room of the Union by J. P. Piper Esq., deputy coroner on view of the body of Emma R. Hills, an infant who died under circumstances detailed in the following report of the evidence. Mr. John Andrews was foreman of the jury, and amongst those who witnessed the proceedings were Capt. Jackson, Mr. Scoles, and Mr. Stewardson.

'Mrs. Ann Wood, wife of a labourer in Gravel Lane, identified the body as that of Emma Rebecca Hills, whose mother lodged with witness for about five months until she went into the Union, about a fortnight last Wednesday. During that time the mother suckled the child and used to give it sop, as the baby used to refuse milk. The baby was "a poor little mortal" when it came to witness's house and did not look as if it would live. The mother was not in good health, as she had not half enough of food. Sometimes the mother paid her rent (1s a week) and sometimes it was paid by her daughter who lived away from here. The mother was unable to do work, but used to go on small errands, and was apparently fond of the child, for she used to treat it kindly and never let it cry if she could. About three or four days before she went into the Union she called in Mr. Goldsmith's assistant, who said the child was starving and recommended that the mother should go to the Workhouse. Never saw the mother give the child a cordial, but while the mother was out the Witness had got port wine for the child.

'Mr. Smith, M.R.C.E., Assistant to Mr. Goldsmith deposed that on the morning of the 6th Sept. he saw the child, which was very much emaciated indeed. He inquired whether it had been a long time ill, and was told by the mother that it had been wasting away for some months. He next asked her how the child had been fed, and was told that it had been fed chiefly on sop [bread soaked in a liquid], the mother not having had much milk. Came to the conclusion that the child had not had sufficient nourishment, and told them medicine was now of no use. Gave last witness a certificate for Mr. Priest, Relieving Officer, to the effect that the child was dying for the want of food. On the left side of the child's head there were eruptive sores, common to children badly nourished. Saw the child being fed with sop and it took it, but not eagerly. Practically the child had been starving from birth for the mother was not fed sufficiently, her earnings, as she said, being only 4d. a day. The child had had sufficient food to fill the stomach but not food of a sufficiently nourishing nature. Had seen the child since its death, and found abscesses on the right wrist and the ancle [ankle] which were not there when he had seen the child alive. The mother appeared to be suffering from starvation.

'Catherine Horton, nurse at the Union, deposed: The deceased and her mother entered the Workhouse on the 7th inst., the child looking very emaciated. It was fed daily on milk, arrowroot and wine, and was also suckled by the mother. After the first two days the child took to its food better, but got worse during the last two days, during which it took very little food. It was treated very kindly by its mother, and was attended to by Dr. Prior. The child died on the morning of the 16th inst. The mother had not sufficient nourishment for the child.

'Julia Hills (46) mother of the deceased, was also examined, and deposed: I am a single woman. The deceased was 12 months on the 5th Sept. but has never been healthy and has always been weakly. I have fed it on sop, not having sufficient for it, and it took the sop willingly, three or four cups a day. Sometimes I used to earn 1s. a day and sometimes not 2s a week, and had to pay 1s. a week for lodgings. I have never given the child any opium or cordials but have given it some gin.

'By a juror: I was confined of this child in the Union, but it was very weak from its birth.

'Verdict from **natural causes**.'

This is a truly shocking case. How could anyone allow a mother and child to suffer from starvation until the death of this twelve-month-old little girl. Given gin, port wine and 'sop' for nourishment it is surprising that she survived for a year or so. Was there no public information and guidance for mothers at the time, to ensure the safety of mother and child? Gravel Lane is off Midland Road at the rear of River Street, and this is only a stone's throw from the Infirmary where mother and child could have obtained help, and why did the mother not enter the Work-house sooner for her sake and her baby's. The only positive I see here is that the mother, Julia Hills, declared that she had never given her infant daughter opium! Were there no charities such as the Salvation Army, which could have offered help in such cases? If only we could rewind time and educate in order to avoid such horrors.

The burial of little Emma took place in Bedford Cemetery, grave plot H.10.266 and this was followed by a further burial in the same plot, of a five-year-old boy on 11 October 1870.

God bless them both.

Sources:

The Bedford Times and Bedfordshire Independent September 27 1870 p.8 Burial in Bedford Cemetery grave ref. H.10.266.

THE CHARGE OF CHILD MURDER
AT TILBROOK

George Newman Haynes

It was in November of 1881 that news broke concerning deaths in the Haynes' household in the village of Tilbrook. The following is a reproduction of the article carried by the local newspaper:

'On Friday the 11th Inst. [instant], at Sharnbrook Divisional Petty Sessions, before Mr. H. H. Green (in the chair); Mr. T. Bagnall, Mr. L. G. S. Gibbard, and Mr. E. S. Watson, with the Clerk, Mr. J. Garrard, Jane Haynes wife of Thomas Richard Haynes, was charged with the wilful murder of her infant son, George Newman Haynes, on the 8th inst.

'Mr. Clare appeared to watch the case on behalf of the accused.

'Elizabeth Gell, a single woman of Tilbrook stated that she lived near Mr. Haynes' house. He was a Corporal in the Royal Engineers, and she had known his wife about a fortnight. They had two children, both boys, one being about three or four years of age and the other, the deceased, about ten months. On Monday, the 7th inst., witness had the care of the children. At about ten o'clock Mr. Haynes came to her and asked her to look after the children as his wife seemed very strange in her manner. Witness then took charge of the children until the mother got a little better. She went to the house with Mr. Haynes, and on arriving there, saw Mrs. Haynes who said "good morning," and asked her to see to the children for her. Witness said she would, brought the children away and took them to her own home. On Tuesday she took them back and saw Mrs. Haynes who asked her what sort of a night she had had. Witness said it was middling, and Mrs. Haynes observed that she did not think the child was very well, perhaps it was cutting its teeth. After witness had held the boy for a few minutes Mrs. Haynes took him out of her arms and hushed him to sleep. It had been very restless all night. Witness went upstairs to fetch something for the wash, and Mrs. Haynes accompanied her taking also the little boy. Witness afterwards returned to her house, the biggest boy going with her. When upstairs Mrs. Haynes asked her to lay the blankets straight on the bed, and witness did. The accused placed her child on the bed and witness took the clothes, went downstairs and returned home, leaving Mrs. Haynes with the child. She did not see the child again until the day of the inquest when it was dead. About midday on Tuesday the 8th inst., she again went to Mrs. Haynes' house. The accused was sitting in a chair downstairs. Witness thought her mind was queer and asked where the child was? She said it was sleeping. Witness replied "It is having a good sleep then." Mrs. Haynes said "Yes it is." Witness suggested that she should bring the child to her house when it awoke, and Mrs. Haynes assented. After stopping about five minutes witness came away, and did not go upstairs. About 7 or 8 o'clock on Tuesday night she saw Mrs. Haynes in the yard; her husband and several people were also present; they said the child was dead. On Monday Mrs. Haynes was very strange in her talk saying that she was no mother to the child. She cried very much, but did not complain of being ill, nor did she find fault with any one. During the previous week witness saw that Mrs. Haynes' conduct was peculiarly strange; she wandered about the house and wrung her hands.

'Thomas Richard Haynes, a corporal in the Royal Engineers stationed at Tilbrook, said he had been in that village about a month, and the deceased child was ten months old. His wife had been strange in her manner for the last ten months, since, in fact, the child was born. At her confinement, which took place at Bedford, she was attended by Mrs. Lodovick, a midwife, of Hassett-street. His wife came to Tilbrook at the same time that he did. After her confinement she was attended by Mr. Kinsey, surgeon, for a white leg, [also known as milk leg and relates to diseases associated with deep vein thrombosis, often seen in mothers who had recently given birth] and for ten or twelve weeks she remained under his treatment. She had never been very strong and scarcely had any appetite. A few days after coming to Tilbrook he noticed that she was strange in her manner, the children were neglected and meals were not prepared. On one occasion she said to him "I am your ruination." On Monday the 8th her strangeness was still more apparent, and he therefore sent for Miss Gell to come and fetch the children. On Monday his wife came to the White Horse for him, and stayed with Mrs. Bradley, the Landlady, in the afternoon. About five o'clock she left for Miss Gell. However, she did not stop there, and promised

Mrs. Bradley to come back the same day. Witness went for her and about nine o'clock Mrs. Bradley suggested that they should stay there all night. On Tuesday morning his wife seemed as usual and they left at about ten minutes to eight. As they were crossing a stile on the way home, Mrs. Haynes got on the top of the stile with both feet and jumped forward. On alighting she fell backwards into the mud and seemed very vexed with herself. When they got home the children were still with Miss Gell. At nine o'clock he left home and went to Covington in pursuit of his ordinary duties, and did not come back until four in the afternoon. He called at Mrs. Bradley's and was told that his wife had been to see him. He went home and she met him at the door and said "I have killed little Georgie; I have cut his throat and he is lying upstairs". Witness said "You don't mean to tell me you have killed the child?" and she said "Yes, send for a policeman." She then got a lucifer, [a friction match, Lucifer being Latin for light-bringer] and lit the lamp, saying "Don't be afraid, the child won't hurt you," and she went upstairs before him with the light. In the room she said "Poor little thing; I have kissed him a dozen times since I cut his throat." Witness found that the child was lying on its right side, and his wife added, "I did not hurt it at all; I got it to sleep. Never mind; you will have a bright future before you now; don't worry." About a fortnight ago when he went home he found Mrs. Haynes had been trying to hang herself with a piece of rope, and she produced a written statement to that effect, exonerating her husband.

'P.s. Clark deposed to going to the house, and that Mrs. Haynes said to him, "I killed the child this morning sometime before dinner. I got it to sleep, laid it down on the bed, and cut its throat, and I don't think it moved afterwards; I did not see it." She then went to a box and produced the razor, handed it to him, and it was the same as the one then in the possession of the Court. She said that was the razor she used. Witness apprehended her and took her to Sharnbrook station. She accompanied him willingly.

'Mr. Henry Arthur Hallett, surgeon, Kimbolton, stated that he was called upon about six o'clock to go to Tilbrook, and on visiting the cottage of Corporal Haynes, he found the child quite dead and cold. It was in an inner room upstairs, lying on its right side, with a wound in front of the neck, right down to the bone, such as would have been inflicted by a razor. Death must have ensued quickly.

'In answer to the charge, Mr. Clare, on behalf of the Mrs. Haynes, said the defence was reserved.

'The accused was then committed for trial at the Assizes. No bail was applied for.'

A similar article appeared in the *South Wales Echo*, Friday 19 November 1881:

Murder by a Mother

'A coroners inquiry held at Tilbrook, a small village on the borders of Bedfordshire, into the circumstances attending the death of George Haynes, aged 10 months, resulted in a verdict of wilful murder being returned against the mother, Jane Haynes, wife of a second corporal in the Royal Engineers, engaged with a survey party in the neighbourhood. Ever since the birth of the child the mother has appeared strange at intervals, and only a day before the child was killed the father placed it and another son in the care of a neighbour. Shortly before the child was found dead the mother had been fondling it. By her own confession, however, it appears that she got the baby off to sleep, held it on the bed, and then cut its throat. It was found on the floor upstairs by the father quite dead. When apprehended the poor woman was in terrible agony, and said she loved the child dearly, and could not think what possessed her when she did the act.'

Post-natal depression (puerperal-mania) may well have been the cause of this poor lady's condition, which led to infanticide and the loss of the child she said she loved dearly. She clearly needed medical attention and support, which might have averted the tragedy. She was found "not guilty on the grounds of insanity" and the judge directed that the prisoner be detained during her Majesty's pleasure.

Jane Haynes was committed to Broadmoor and transferred there from Bedford Prison. It is known that she was still there in 1917, aged c.61 years. Her first-born son Thomas Richard Haynes went to America in 1894 and became an American national on 25 January 1902. He was drafted into the American forces in 1917 and fought in the first World War. He returned to America in 1922 on the 'President Adams'.

Sources:

The Bedfordshire Times and Independent, 19 November 1881 p. 6
The South Wales Echo, Friday 19 November 1881 p.2
Collins English Dictionary
Ancestry Library Edition.co.uk
US WW1 Draft Registration Card

GALLANT RESCUES FROM DROWNING IN BEDFORD

Emma, Ester and Wiliam Clarke

It is very surprising to hear of a rescue from drowning in this period, and even more so the rescue of three children by one very brave person.

'On Sunday morning an event occurred which, looked at from whatever point of view, seems to be as worthy of honourable recognition as any hitherto brought under the notice of societies whose function it is to reward and hold up for emulation deeds of well-directed bravery. A lath-render named Thomas Farmer, in the employ of Messrs. Green, and residing at Bedesman's-place, has saved, at imminent risk to his own life, and at some little injury to his health, three little children from a watery grave.

'It appears that at about half ten on Sunday morning three children – William Clarke, aged 13, Esther Clarke, 5, and Emma Clarke, 3, living in Bedesman's-place were, with others, playing near the mill-race of Mr. Harrison's Flour Mill. A low wall separates the stream from the road, and a high hoarding formerly prevented persons from falling over. A flood washed away part of the hoarding, and a balk of timber has been placed in the gap. Anglers and small children, however, persist in getting over the obstruction, not-withstanding frequent cautions as to the danger they incur. Mr. Harrison and others have several times driven away the children, but they as often return, and it would seem that the parents themselves are not given to over-carefulness in the matter.

'At the spot indicated the water is from eight to ten feet in depth, but more probably the former at the time in question, when, it should be added, the mill was fortunately not going. The youngest child, Emma, tumbled in first, and the boy, William, in attempting to catch her, was also dragged in. Then the girl, Esther, in endeavouring to help her brother, also fell in. All three sank and would assuredly have been drowned but for the circumstances we are about to describe. The screams of the children on the bank attracted the attention of Thomas Farmer and a companion named Thomas Wright, who were in the backyard of their house some 180 yards away. Both men at once ran to the spot, and Farmer, divining what was the matter, divested himself of his coat and other encumbering clothing on the way. On arriving Farmer, without hesitation, plunged into the water, dived, and soon reappeared with the girl Emma, whom he handed to Wright, who, not being able to swim, was standing on the bank, but there proved very useful. The spot where the boy had sunk was then pointed out. Farmer again dived and recovered the body, which was handed to Wright. Farmer partly got out, not knowing that there was another child still in the water. The mother then ran up in a frantic state of mind, and exclaimed, "There's another one," at the same time a hat was observed by Farmer floating on the water. Thoroughly exhausted, Farmer appealed to the bystanders, asking if any of them could swim, but it appeared they could not and were unwilling to undertake the risk. He again took the plunge, and after some moments' absence came to the surface with the missing girl, who was then carried home in an unconscious condition.

'Insp. Haymen and others then came up, and efforts were made to restore consciousness but the same time they were in vain. Meanwhile Mr. Robinson, surgeon, was sent for and he at once despatched his assistant who, on his arrival applied the approved methods of reviving animation under such circumstances, working the arms backwards and forwards to induce respiration. Under the prompt treatment of an unknown bystander the child had already partly recovered consciousness, and she was soon pronounced out of danger. At the time the eldest and youngest of the children seemed little worse for the ducking, but we hear that the boy has since suffered from shock to the system. Farmer was unable to attend his work on Tuesday on account of some indisposition arising from his having plunged into the water while in a heated condition caused by his running. He is, we understand, an expert swimmer and diver. It is said that he once before saved a man's life at Wisbeach. The recent incident in which he has played so conspicuous a part will therefore sufficiently illustrate the utility of indulging in such exercises or of acquiring some practical knowledge of the natatory [swimming] art.

'The matter is, as it assuredly deserves to be, laid before the Royal Humane Society, and we sincerely endorse the wish that it may be suitably dealt with.'

.

Duck Mill (Harrison's Flour Mill) c. 1880

It is easy to see why this area close to Bedesman's-place attracted young people, with the mill itself, an open grassed leisure area, a roller skating rink and the river. However, much to the Writer's frustration no evidence of the family living in this area can be found, despite the detail given in the article. With no trace of the family, no deaths and burial details can be found [at any time following this event]. It may be concluded that they were visiting Bedford at the time of the incident. If they were Bedford residents then they would most likely have ended their days in Bedford Cemetery.

Despite failing to trace this family, the article serves to highlight just one other almost fatal accident and a most incredible rescue which saved three young lives.

'Another rescue from drowning, which took place on the same day at twenty minutes to five in the afternoon, was equally successful, though perhaps the circumstances did not call for the same display of self-sacrifice. A little girl named Florence Bush, aged 5, residing in Lime-street, fell off the embankment wall into the river. The water was not very deep, but older persons have been drowned in a less depth, and to a little girl, terrified by the situation, the accident could have proved fatal, had not Mr. Goatley promptly came from the other side in a boat, and, with the assistance of P.c. Askew, got the child out. Florence then went home with her sister, but otherwise seemed little worse for the wetting.'

Duck Mill

This article illustrates once again the grave dangers posed by the river. One wonders why compulsory secondary education did not include on the curriculum, instruction in swimming. Thomas Farmer was indeed a most courageous man, and it was only thanks to him that Emma, Ester and William Clarke survived.

Source:

The Bedfordshire Times and Independent, Saturday 12 August, 1882, p. 6

Photographs:

Maurice Nicholson and Linda Ayres, origin unknown

SINGULAR INFANT MORTALITY

Thomas Newman

There follows yet another sad story from April 1880:

'On Monday afternoon the borough coroner (Dr. Prior) held an enquiry at the Angel Inn, Cauldwell-street, Bedford, into the circumstances attending the death of Thomas Newman, the infant son of Thomas and Mary Newman of Bridewell-yard, St. Mary's.

'The coroner explained to the jury (Mr. Richards foreman) that the sudden death of this infant came to the knowledge of the police. From enquiries that had since been made it appeared that this was a legitimate child, but there had been a singular mortality in the same family, and therefore he considered it right that an inquest should be held. The following evidence was then taken:-

'Mary Ann Richardson, living in Bridewell-Yard, wife of Benjamin Richardson, labourer, deposed that the body viewed by the Jury was that of Thomas Newman, son of Thomas Newman, a labourer. Witness lived next door to Mr. Newman. She had known deceased about six weeks, since she resided in the yard, and had seen him frequently. It was a thin delicate child. There had not been much alteration in him since. He was always wrapped up and cared for. The child looked as if he were going in a consumption. He had had no medical attendance that she knew of. Saturday morning witness noticed an alteration. On

Sunday morning at four o'clock, the mother called witness up. She went into Mr. Newman's house, when Mrs. Newman said, "I think my baby is worse." Witness took the child from her and kept it in her arms until it died. Its breathing was very bad when she took it. The child got gradually worse, and died about 20 minutes past five. It had the whooping cough and went off in a fit of coughing. The Newmans had two other children living. Dr. Johnson attended Mrs. Newman at her confinement. She knew nothing of the family previous to her residence in Bridewell-yard.

'Mary Newman, mother of the deceased, deposed that herself and her husband had lived in Bridewell-yard about four years. They came from Biggleswade to Bedford. She had had 12 children altogether, two of whom were now living. Two or three of them were still born and some only lived two or three days. The last who died was 9 months old all but a week. No inquest had ever been held on any of her children before. She had had a medical certificate in every case except the present. Deceased was born 10 weeks last Sunday morning, when born it appeared to be a beautiful baby. At the end of five weeks the cough came upon him and he turned black in the face several times and vomited blood. A week last Sunday she sent her daughter for Mr. Johnson. Witness received a message that he could not come, because she had not paid him. She made no other attempt to obtain medical assistance. Mr. Peer, the relieving officer, had several times refused her husband medical assistance when he made application for it. On Sunday morning, about 4 o'clock deceased was taken with a fit of coughing. There was no change until this time. Witness did not like the look of her child and called in her next-door neighbour, Mrs. Richardson, who held the baby until it died, that was say in about one hour and 20 minutes. In reply to the foreman witness said the child had had no medicine whatever. She had given it some Spanish Liquorice, which was boiled with some clover-hay, as the doctor advised her. She gave the child some milk sop.

'In reply to the coroner witness said she had had three children born in Bedford. They were all dead. Before this child, the two children were attended by Dr. Goldsmith, one died when it was about 10 weeks old, the other was 9 months old when it died. Dr. Goldsmith gave her the certificate for the child who died at 9 months. She forgot what the disease was that this child died from. In the second case, of the child before the present, Dr. Goldsmith gave a certificate which was to the effect that the child died from ulcerated bowels.

'Dr. C. G. Johnson, Harpur-street, deposed that in December of last year he was engaged to attend Mrs. Newman in what he understood to be her third confinement. He was told distinctly that this was the third child and produced a memoranda book in which this was recorded. Deceased was a healthy child when born and did well until he left them in about 12 days. Shortly after this he was called to see the husband who was suffering from bronchitis and when attending him the mother told witness that the child was not well. There were two other children in the house that had whooping cough; he heard them coughing. He visited the man two or three times and told them if they wanted any future attendance they must enter the dispensary. Since then he had heard nothing of the family and had not since seen deceased until this afternoon. He had made an external examination of the deceased and found no marks upon the body. The child was considerably thinner than when born but not more than would be due to whooping cough. He would not term it emaciated. The appearances were not inconsistent with death from whooping cough. It was correct that he ordered boiled clover for deceased about six weeks since as a kind of domestic remedy.

'The mother recalled, said the two children in the house were not hers but Mrs. Cox's. Her son was in the Militia Band and her daughter lived at home with her.

'The coroner having reviewed the evidence the jury returned a verdict of "Death from Natural Causes."'

Bridewell-Yard

Ten dead children in one family is tragic; little or no medical attention, and nothing more than a 'domestic remedy' suggested by the doctor. Whooping cough, bronchitis, ulcerated bowels and who knows what else. Poverty played a large part in this dreadful outcome, with parents struggling to exist and in no way able to support twelve children. Impoverished living conditions as the picture of Bridewell-yard illustrates, condemned the occupants to poor health. Boiled clover for a dying infant, Spanish Liquorice, milk sop and a miserable wait for nature to take its cruel course. Such children had no chance of a life.

Sources:

The Bedfordshire Times and Independent, Saturday 17 April 1880 p.6
Burial ref: 41-G9, Burial Register 8 page 19 entry 92
Date of burial 16 April 1880, age 10 months

Photograph:

Maurice Nicholson

DROWNED OFF THE EMBANKMENT

William Ingrey

Little William lived in an impoverished area of St Mary's, quite close to the river.

'A sad case of drowning occurred on Monday evening [23 December] down the Embankment. A little boy named William Ingrey, living in Bedeman's-place [St Mary's] was running along the low parapet opposite the Town and County Club, when he accidentally fell into the river. Another boy who was with him ran home to convey the news - no-one else being near at the time – and by the time the poor little fellow was got out life was extinct. The inquest was held at the King's Arms Inn on Tuesday, before Dr. Prior, Borough Coroner, and J. Pugh, R. Goatley, A. Thurley, E. Eccles, H. Steers, C. Rubythorn, G.Setchell, J. Perkins, and F. Sinfield.

'The Coroner remarked that the child was drowned in a public part of the river on the previous evening. He did not know that the evidence they would get would be satisfactory, but they must judge how the accident occurred. Perhaps some of the jury had noticed that the river was being dragged again in the same spot that afternoon, it being alleged that a little girl had fallen off the Embankment, as previous they would exercise their thoughts, as previous juries had done, as to whether the protection to the river at this point was sufficient. If any recommendation on the matter emanated from the jury, he would convey it to the proper quarter.

'Elizabeth Ashwell said she resided at No 1 Bedesman's-place with Mrs. Ingrey, The body shown to the jury was that of William Ingrey, who was seven years old, and he was the son of Edward Ingrey, confectioner. Witness last saw the boy alive at a quarter to five on Monday afternoon. She told him the tea was ready and that he must not go away, but he went out. Witness sent a little girl out to fetch him in but she returned and said she could not see him. Witness went out to look for him and saw a little boy who told her the deceased had just fallen in the river. Witness asked him whereabouts, and he replied. "Opposite the Club." Witness then went down the Embankment and saw the deceased in the water nearly opposite the Club. He was floating face downwards and she could just see his back. Witness saw Mr. Webb and asked him to get deceased out of the water. Mr. Webb went to Biffen's boat stand, came back with a boat, and got out the deceased. She saw the deceased brought to Goatley's boatyard and she helped to carry him home. He appeared dead. In answer to the foreman, witness said it was about twenty minutes from the time the boy left the house to when she saw him in the water.

'Ralph Berrington, a boy aged nine, was the next witness called but he was not sworn. In answer to questions he stated that about a quarter to five on Monday he went with deceased into the Duck Mill Recreation Ground, over the suspension bridge and up the Embankment. When they got to the stone Embankment the deceased ran along the kerb, and witness shouted to him "Don't go on there; come on off." Deceased however still kept running on, and when opposite the Club he slipped off all at once, into the water. It was dark and nobody was near, so witness ran home and told Elizabeth Ashwell.

'Mr. W. H. Biffen said that on the previous afternoon he was having his tea about ten minutes past five, when a knock came at the door. Mrs. Biffen answered it and was told by Mr. Webb that a child was in the water and had been over five minutes and would Mr. Biffen get a boat and get it out. Witness immediately went out and got a boat and with Master Frank Corry-Smith rowed to and found the child about 25 ft. from the wall floating with just the back part of the head above water. Witness lifted the deceased carefully into the boat and told Corry-Smith to row to the steps. In the meantime witness undid the boys clothes and found the body quite warm. He tried artificial respiration, and on reaching the steps he lifted the body out and laid it down. With Corry-Smith's help, witness continued to move the arms up and down, rubbed the chest, and occasionally laid the body on one side. When Dr. Sharpin arrived he examined the body by the light of some lucifers, and pronounced him dead. The deceased was taken across the water to Goatley's boatyard and witness saw no more of him.,

'Mr. H. W. Sharpin, surgeon, stated that on the previous evening about 5.20 a policeman came to his house and told him a child had just been got out of the river; and asked him to go and see it. He at once went with him and found a child that had recently [been] taken out of the water lying on the steps at the bridge. Witness examined the body by match-light and it was quite evident the child had been dead some time. Witness would have said that from the appearance of the body the child had been under the water at least five minutes and probably longer. There was some foam on the mouth and nostrils and the face was livid.

'The jury at once returned a verdict of Accidental Death, and the Foreman remarked that now was the time for the jury to consider whether they should make any recommendation as to the unprotected state of the Embankment.

'The Coroner said he remembered holding at least three Inquests on persons who had accidentally fallen off the Embankment into the river, and there had been several suicides.

'Mr. Biffen informed the jury that since he had lived on the Embankment he had been in the river several times to fetch people out and he and his men who looked after the boats had been the means of getting scores of people with boats. The high part of the Embankment was more dangerous than the low part because people falling from it struggled outwards into deep water whereas lower down the water was shallower, and if anyone slipped in he could be reached and soon pulled out. Some of the persons he had rescued were in a more or less exhausted state, and many of them were children. He had seen children racing along this parapet, and at the least stumble they might fall into the river.

'The Foreman said he had often warned children to come off the high parapet near the bridge. That little piece of work cost £700, so it would cost about £4,000 to continue it right along the Embankment. Even if this were done, children could get on it, and he thought an unclimeable [unclimbable] fence would be much the best.'Mr. H. Steers suggested a 4ft. Iron fence with spear heads. The Foreman said this agreed with his view, and he thought a fence ought to be erected immediately. He had often seen servants and ladies leading children along the parapet, and he thought it was foolish on their part, because if the children were there alone they would [be] sure to run along it again and they might fall in the river.

'Another juryman remarked that if some big "swell" [a distinguished person] were to accidentally fall over the Embankment and get drowned there would soon be a stir made about it and the fence would then be erected.

'On the proposition of the Foreman, seconded by Mr. H. Steers, the following resolution was unanimously adopted, and the Coroner said he would forward it to the Corporation:- "The jury are of opinion that the present unprotected state of the river along the Embankment is a constant source of danger, as shown by several accidents fatal and non-fatal, and beg earnestly to represent to the Town Council that a proper fence is required."'

The authorities, in spite of all the evidence and preventable loss of life, are dragging their feet and are more concerned with cost than the protection of local people, and children in particular, it would appear.

Sources:

The Bedfordshire Standard, Saturday December 28, 1889
Died 23 December 1889 and buried 27 December 1889 aged 7

Known as William but most likely Edward William.

CHILD SCALDED TO DEATH

Mabel Leadbeater

The Bedford Record, 28 September 1889 reported as follows:

'At the Infirmary on Tuesday the Borough Coroner (Dr. Prior) held an inquiry into the circumstances attending the death of Mabel Leadbeater, the infant daughter of John Leadbeater, gamekeeper, of Pulloxhill, who was admitted to the Infirmary on Saturday suffering from severe scalds, and who died on Sunday from the effects of the injuries. The following composed the jury: - Messrs. T. Minney (foreman), G. Finch, C. Catlin, E. Yorke, J. Gill, J. Dudley, W. H. Johnson, and E. Dracup. The following was the evidence:-

'Eliza Leadbeater, wife of John Leadbeater, Game-keeper, of Pulloxhill, and mother of the child, identified the body, and said the child was nine months old. On Saturday morning witness tied the child in her high chair and left her to go up stairs. The chair stood by the side of the fire, and on the fire was a saucepan containing hot water. Witness had not been upstairs above five minutes, when she heard the chair fall. She ran down immediately, picked up the baby, who was on the floor, undressed her, and attended to her. Witness saw that the saucepan was knocked down and that the baby was scalded, and she supposed she fell forward in trying to reach the handle of the saucepan.

Witness procured some oil and wadding, with which she dressed the child, and she then wrapped her in a blanket and brought her at once to the Infirmary. The house surgeon wished her to leave the child in the Infirmary, but she felt she could not, and she only took her to a friend's in Althorpe-street. However, she took the child back to the Infirmary two or three hours afterwards and left her there

'Dr. Skelding, house surgeon, said the deceased was brought to the Infirmary about one o'clock on Saturday by her mother. He found her suffering from severe scalds on the back, the side of the face, the back of the head, the back of the arms, and one leg. The child was in a very exhausted condition, and he advised that she should be kept in the Infirmary, but the mother was anxious to take her home. The wounds were dressed and the child was well wrapped up. The mother took her away, but returned about four o'clock and left her. Deceased remained in an exhausted state, became gradually worse, and died the next afternoon. Death was occasioned by the injuries received.

'The jury returned a verdict of Accidental Death.'

No doubt the mother must have panicked after witnessing the child's serious injuries, probably not sure what to do, and being quite some distance from the Infirmary. Specialists of the period recommended in 'The Treatment of Burns' [The British Medical 1876] for burns and scalds the exclusion of air from the wound to allay pain by opiates, Goulard-water with laudanum, painting the surface with ink or covering it with whitewash or similar, which will crust and exclude air, common flour thickly dredged on more superficial burns or some oily substance, or calamine, Carron oil made by mixing lime water and linseed oil, and carbonised oil, among other remedies. I wonder how many mothers were aware of these remedies or had such things to hand? This was a sad, painful and shocking death for a nine-month old baby.

Source:

The Bedford Record, 28 September 1889
The Treatment of Burns, The British Medical Journal Vol. 2, No. 815, August 12 1876

DEATH OF AN APPRENTICE

William Norris

It was Tuesday 28 August 1877 and in a shed in Ram Yard at the rear of 57 High Street, Bedford, work was proceeding as normal with two young men – William Norris being only 17 years of age, the other aged 20 and married with a child – busy filling cartridges with gunpowder. The older man had completed his apprenticeship with Mr. Adkin, Gunsmith; William had begun his apprenticeship some one and a half years earlier, a single young man living with his family at 69 St. Mary's. Among other employees was a 12 year old lad, Charles Johnson of Chandos-street, a boy whose job it was to carry gunpowder and shot across the yard to the men engaged in filling cartridges in the shed. What a responsibility for a 12 year old child!

Without warning an explosion occurred which it is said could be heard as far away as Goldington, and the two young men received the full force of the shock in their chests and faces. Neighbours bravely ran up the passage leading from the High Street to the scene of the explosion to offer assistance. With clothes on fire William was taken to Mr. Sergeant's shop and the second man to the Lion Hotel bar. William's wounds were treated with linseed oil [to keep out the air]. The most badly affected areas were wrapped in Tow [coarse hemp or flax] saturated with oil. These young men suffered greatly, their hair was singed off close to the skin, eyebrows and eye lashes burnt right off, bodies charred black with soot and fire, skin breaking off in patches and smouldering with a sickening odour as the oil was applied. Even William's socks were on fire when he was helped into the shop. The explosion shattered windows at the rear of the shop and disarranged furniture and goods.

Obviously both of these young men must have been in shock and in great pain but they were able to walk, with support, after about twenty minutes, a few steps to the cab which took them to the Infirmary, escorted by a Mr. Fryer of St. Lloyes, who accompanied them, Charles wrapped in a sheet, William in a blanket. Charles suffered the worst injuries it seems and his hands were badly burnt; the report mentions 'raw flesh' which speaks of the severity of the injuries. He died the following day at 9.30 pm. William was said to be 'progressing favourably' but nevertheless he too died on Tuesday 4 September at about 4.30, almost exactly a week after the accident.

Subsequently an inquiry and inquest was held to determine the cause of the explosion. The report states that with each gunpowder explosion an inquiry must be held and a rigorous inquiry at the inquest on the deceased. Mr. Adkin who is not mentioned in the rescue expressed his gratitude to those who helped at a time when he was too agitated to have effectually intervened himself. He stated that he was in the front shop at the time of the explosion. [He was their employer and owner of the shop and business].

The inquiry took place on Thursday 6 September. The jury viewed the body of William at the General Infirmary mortuary, where 'the body of the deceased presented a hideous mass of burning all over the face, neck and arms' and further burns to his legs and ankles. The coroner adjourned the inquiry until the 19 September at the Corn Exchange, and issued a certificate for burial, which took place. William and the other unfortunate young man were both buried in Bedford Cemetery. Charles Paxton of Midland Road was given a 'military funeral' which took place on Monday 3 September. In addition to leaving a wife and child, he was also supporting his widowed mother. A collection was held for his family. William's funeral took place on 7 September 1877 and it is sad indeed that no collection was made for him. He was also helping to support his family and would have done so for many years during his working life no doubt. The Inquiry concluded as follows:

'The jury find that Charles Paxton and William Norris came by their deaths through injuries received by an accidental explosion of gunpowder on the premises of Mr. Henry Adkin on the 28th of August, but how such explosion was caused there is not sufficient evidence to show.

'The said jury are further of the opinion that the occupier of the premises has failed to enforce the necessary precautions against accidents; and

'That efficent [efficient] supervision has not been kept up by the local authority through its inspecting officer

'We wish also to state that, in the opinion of the jury, the storage of large quantities of gunpowder and the manufacture of cartridges in such a crowded locality is perilous to the public.'

There is so much detail about this accident in the newspapers of the time. The interesting thing is how so many traders in the industry rushed to register their premises after this tragedy:

'Sept. 5 Mr. William Burr, ironmonger, Silver-street and Cook-street, gunpowder; Sept. 8 Mr. Hy Adkin, gunmaker, High-street, mixed explosives; Sept. 10, the executors of the late Mr. R. Graves, High-street, grocer, gunpowder; Sept. 11 Mr. Joseph Frazer, ironmonger, Silver-street, gunpowder; Sept. 13 Mr. Edward L. Moulton, iron-monger, High-street, gunpowder.'

Central Bedford would seem to have been rather a dangerous place back in 1877!

In addition to newspaper reports which featured news of the accident is a great deal of information concerning the proceedings which followed.

Mr. Henry Adkin, Gunmaker and the employer of these unfortunate young men died 1 May 1914 aged 93.

Sources:

Bedfordshire Times & Independent, Saturday 1 September 1877 p.5
Bedfordshire Times & Independent, Saturday 8 September 1877
Bedfordshire Times & Independent, Saturday 15 September 1877
Bedfordshire Times & Independent, Saturday 22 September 1877 Grave ref: William Norris H.3 178, Charles Paxton E.7 206,
Henry Adkin E.4/13

A CHILD DROWNED AT BEDFORD

William Mardell

This little tale relates to a child of four years of age wandering the streets by the river with no parental supervision, as is so often the case, it seems:

'An inquest was held at the Nag's Head, Midland-road, before Dr. C. E. Prior, borough coroner, on Monday morning on the body of a child named William Mardle, whose parents reside in Maitland-street, Bedford, and who was drowned on the previous Saturday afternoon. The following were sworn on the Jury:- Mr. S. Chetham (foreman), Messrs. J. Bettison, J Chettle, W. Norris, A. Smith, J. Andrews, W. Gurney, W. Pedder, W. Skerman, T. Linford, J. Barber, R. Franklin, J. Ash.

'Elizabeth Buck, a neighbour of the parents of the deceased, said she saw the child on Saturday at about 3 o'clock. He was then walking towards the cattle market. The child was nearly five years of age, and his father was a telegraph linesman employed by the Midland Railway Company. About half an hour afterwards a boy came to Mrs. Mardle and said her boy was in the water, so witness at once ran to the bank of the river at Batt's Ford. She saw the cap of the deceased in the river some distance off and soon afterwards saw his head. Someone from Mr. Chethams came and got the child out. Her little boy, who was with the deceased, had told her that the child was trying to get his cap out of the water when he fell in.

'William Coleman, in the employ of Mr. Chetham, deposed to going to the river where he saw the body. He jumped in the water and took it out, but the child was quite dead.

'Dr. Adams said on Saturday afternoon about 4.20 he reached the residence of deceased, having been summoned there from the other side of the bridge, where he happened to be. He found the body lying partially dressed on the bed. The child was perfectly dead, and he should think had been dead an hour or thereabouts.

'Mr. Chetham here remarked that he was present when the body was got out and he, with others, tried the usual means for resuscitation but without avail.

'The Jury returned a verdict of "Accidentally Drowned."'

According to the 1871 census Levi Mardle, the child's father, was living with relatives in Luton, unmarried, and a Labourer. In 1881 the census reveals that he was married, aged 35 and living at 31 Maitland Street, Bedford. With him were his wife Sarah Mardle aged 34, Kate E Mardle aged 8 years, [Kate Elizabeth Mardle was buried on 1st April 1882 aged 9] and Rosa, a 7-month-old infant born after the tragic death of her brother William in 1880.

The 1891 census shows the parents still at the same address in Maitland Street living with children Rosa 10, Arthur aged 7, and Harry, 6 months. By1901 the family are still at 31 Maitland Street and we find Rosa aged 20 an Assistant School Mistress, Arthur 17 and a Fishmonger's Assistant, Harry a scholar and a border named Charles Oliver, Assistant Linesman. Finally in 1911 still at the same address, Levi a widower at 63, working as a Telegraph Labourer born in Caddington, Arthur a Fishmonger, Harry Alfred a Brass Moulder's Labourer and Annie Dennis, widow and housekeeper. No doubt Rosa was by then married or perhaps living away from her family and employed as a School Mistress.

There are three graves in Bedford Cemetery, side by side, reference E.2. 137 with two burials, E.2. 146 with two burials and E.2. 155 with one. There are two headstones. William was buried 28th April 1880.

Maitland Street remains, largely unaltered, and is part of the area of Bedford developed from around the 1860s when Bedford Station was opened. This street is comprised terraced and respectable properties. After Levi's move to Bedford and his employment as a Linesman with The Midland Railway, he and his family seem to have prospered, all of the children having found work in the town. They managed to accommodate two borders over time, Charles Oliver and Patrick Galagher (?), boosting the family income. Maitland Street was a short distance from the town centre and the railway station, and No 31 was close to the junction with Midland Road. At the other end of Maitland Street was the cattle market, and beyond that flowed the river. Batts Ford where the witness ran to find the child in the river, was in direct alignment to the Cattle Market and Maitland Street.

It seems incredible that a parent would allow their child to wander alone in the street, down to the Cattle Market and on a few steps to the river. There is no mention of the parents in the article, not even their names. Where were they when the Inquest took place? It does seem strange that it was a neighbour who ran to the child's aid; a child of four years ought never to be exposed to such dangers completely unsupervised. This is such a tragic incident, which is given the briefest of mentions in *The Bedfordshire Times and Independent* article. There is no mention of the funeral service and I believe my research will reveal that there is no gravestone to mark William's short life on this earth. The mere thought of his terrifying death is greatly disturbing.

Rest in peace little William; you are not forgotten.

Sources:

The Bedfordshire Times and Independent, Saturday, 1 May 1880 p.6
Census returns 1871, 1881, 1891, 1901, 1911

INFANTICIDE AT KEMPSTON

Baby Pool

'Rachel Pool (22), lace maker, was charged with the wilful murder of her new-born male child, at Kempston, on the 11th December last [presumed 1869].

'Mr. Abdy, instructed by Mr. James Pearse, solicitor, prosecuted; Mr. Lathom Browne, instructed by Mr. W. A. Stimson, was for the prisoner, who, by permission of His Lordship, was accommodated with a seat in the dock. The following jury was sworn: Septimus Abbott, John Adams, William Bazley, Jonathan Bettles, Frederick Croft, William Rudd Green, Alexander Hawley, Charles Henry Joyce, George Minney, Henry Benjamin Rossoln, Joseph Samuels, George Smith, jun.

'The learned counsel for the prosecution opened the case at considerable length, reviewing all the facts and urging the jury to decide upon the evidence about to be brought before them.

'Letitia Keep, wife of Amos Keep, Kempston, deposed that she went to prisoner's house on the night of the 11th December last, having been fetched by prisoner's husband, and saw certain marks on the floor. Prisoner was then in bed ill. On December 23rd the prisoner told witness she was sure she had not had a child.

'Cross-examined: Prisoner seemed very ill on the night of the 11th December, and was wrapped up in blankets. She has been married about three years, and her husband left her a little more than a year last harvest. While he was away she used to make lace and keep her father's house. I thought she had had a miscarriage. She has another child, and is very kind to it. Her husband left her because he had not work.

'Rachel, wife of William Farrar, Kempston, deposed that she went to the prisoner's house on Sunday the 12th of December last, about half past one o'clock in the morning. Prisoner was in bed, and stated that she had had a miscarriage. Witness stayed there two hours.

'Not cross-examined.

'Police-constable John Tatman deposed that on Monday 20th December he went to prisoner's house and told her he had called in reference to a rumour that was about the village. She told him she had not been confined and had only a miscarriage. In reply to his questions she stated that it happened on the 11th, and that her husband had gone to Farrar's beerhouse, so that there was no one in the house. When he came home at twenty minutes to ten and saw how bad she was he went for her aunt Keep. She also stated that she had been frightened that afternoon by a dog, and after her husband had gone out she became so ill that she could not move to make anybody hear. On the 23rd December witness searched the premises of the prisoner, with Police-constable Monk, and saw the latter take a bundle out of the privy. It was a bundle tied up in two cloths. Witness untied them and found the body of a male child, with a brick tied up with it. A man's linen collar was tied very tightly around the neck of the child. In an hour or two afterwards witness went again to the prisoner's house, and witness said to the prisoner - "I suppose you are aware that we have taken a child out of your privy?" She replied - "Yes, and no one knows anything about it but myself. No one put it there but myself. I was all alone at the time it was born and was so frightened I did not know what to do. I tied the collar round its neck because I was afraid it would make a noise. It didn't make any noise, but I was afraid it would. I don't think it would, for I believe it would have been strangled. I wrapped it up in a bit of old skirt and put it in a band box. On Sunday morning when my husband was gone to fetch his mother I got up and dressed myself and went and put it in there. I hope they won't punish my husband for it, for he don't know anything at all about it. I done it because I was afraid he would go away again." She had said previously that her husband had told her that if she was in the condition in which people said she was he would live no longer with her, and would go away again. She continued to state - "That time I was with that man he fastened me in the place and I could not get away from him, and I am sure I never was with him only that one." She did not mention the man's name. I took the prisoner into custody afterwards on the charge of concealment of birth.

'Cross-examined: When this long statement was made Jane Smart also was present. The prisoner appeared to have been crying, and was distressed and excited. I don't believe I have omitted any statement she made. I believe in telling her statement to the magistrates I said she used the word "stifled" not "strangled." I now am sure it was the word "stifled." I don't remember whether she said anything to me about the child having been born before she expected. I don't know why her husband left her.

'Jane Smart, single woman, Wood End, Kempston deposed that on the day the body of the child was found she saw the prisoner, and was present when Tatman came. He said to her, "I suppose you know we have found a child in your closet." She said, "I did it myself. It laid on the boards some time and didn't make any noise. I was afraid it would, and so I tied a collar round its neck, because my husband said he would not live with me."

'Cross-examined: It was said to Tatman that the child lay on the boards, and that it was born before she expected.

'Police constable Jonah Monk deposed: I searched the premises on Dec. 23, and found a bundle wrapped in two cloths, one inside the other. There was a child inside and a brick as well, and a man's collar was tied tightly around the child's neck. The child's face lay on the brick, which caused that part of the face to be very black. I took the body to the Cross Keys beer-house, where a post mortem was held on the following day.

'Eliza, the wife of Sergt. Haynes, Borough Police Station, deposed: On the Thursday before Christmas Day the prisoner was in the house. I came down stairs to get her some tea and asked her what they brought her for and she said - "For getting rid of my baby." She said it laid on the boards an hour and never cried. I did not ask her any more then. Later I said to her "You are a married woman, why did you do it?" She replied - "My husband had no work and went away to the Fens. Afterwards he let himself for 7 months as an hostler, [ostler, stableman] and while he was away my father went into a new house. He came to me one day and said he was going out, would I go and clean the house, - there was no workman there. I went, and when I was cleaning the upstairs room, there was a cupboard in the room with some seeds in it, and a workman came up into the room and said - "I have caught you now, my lady," slamming the door to and locking it. I screamed but there was no one near to hear me. My husband came home soon afterwards and heard I was in the family way. He said if it was so he would go away again and never live with me any more. I begged it might happen when he was not at home, and I thought if I got rid of it I would not be found out. I was all alone when it happened. I did not have more than six pains. I thought I heard my husband coming up the yard, so I tied a string round its neck and threw it in the privy. My husband knew nothing of what had happened nor yet my aunt."

'Cross examined: I never cross examined a witness in such a manner before. I asked those questions out of sympathy, not to extort anything from her. I did so through ignorance, not knowing that I should have to repeat what she told me.

'Mr. G. Robinson, surgeon, Bedford, deposed that he made a post mortem examination in conjunction with Mr. Beechy. He found a collar tied tightly around the neck, and on removing it perceived a deep ecchymose [discolouration of the skin through bruising] impression. The lungs were light red, and when placed in water with the bronchi attached floated very buoyantly. When separate, cut into pieces, and pressed, they still floated very buoyantly. There was a distinct crepitus [crackling chest sound, heard in pneumonia and other conditions] upon pressure. The tongue was black and protruding. The brain and its membrane were very much congested, and the vessels were gorged with blood. My impression is that the child had fully respired. Independent circulation had commenced. The volume of the lungs, their colour, and their floating showed that respiration had taken place. The cause of death I attribute to the constriction of the neck by the collar being tied around it. There was great trouble to get the collar opened, but that might have been owing in a great degree to lying in the fluid.

'Cross-examined: An ecchymose mark can be produced upon a dead body, to a certain extent. I should not have thought the labour in this case was difficult or protracted.

'Mr. F. M. C. Beechey, Kempston, gave corroborative evidence, deposing that from the appearance of the brain principally he was led to believe that death had been caused by strangulation. On the same evening that the post mortem examination had been made, witness had a conversation with the prisoner, who told him that her confinement had been short but sharp.

'Cross-examined: I believe with Dr. Taylor that the hydrostatic [concerned with fluids that are not in motion] test does not enable me to judge whether the child was born alive, but only that it respired. In my opinion the child had breathed. I believe respiration can take place before the child is completely born. The fact of its having respired is not proof of its having been born. A short and painful delivery might produce congestion, blackness of the face, and protrusion of the tongue, but under those circumstances the child would be born dead.' This concluded the case for the prosecution. Mr. Abdy then summed up the main features with his usual ability, and with a marked degree of moderation and kind feeling towards the prisoner.

'Mr. Lathom Browne then addressed the jury as follows: May it please your Lordship, gentlemen of the jury, my learned friend has done, as every English counsel will do, his duty, with moderation and kindness but with justice to his own case as well as that of my client. Thank heavens we have not arrived at the time when we have to fight for a verdict in criminal cases as we do in the civil courts, and therefore, gentlemen, I am permitted by custom and feeling in this country to take a very different tone than what would be consistent with my learned friend's experience. There are many vital points in this case on which you must be satisfied without doubt before you can find a verdict against the prisoner at the bar of guilty of the great crime laid to her charge. You must be satisfied that the child had an independent existence, and that the prisoner at the bar wilfully and of malice afore-thought and knowingly took that life away, and if you are not satisfied on either of these she must stand acquitted by your verdict. I tell you at once I don't stand here to ask you not to find a verdict of concealment, - I should be trying to deceive you and to deceive myself if I did. I have to confine myself solely, gentlemen, to the great charge of murder, and before I deal with the details of the medical evidence I shall ask you to consider what was the position of that woman when this event, whatever it was, took place. She had been left by her husband - I shall use no harsher terms towards him – to live as she could with her first child. She had fallen from her proper state, and was with child when her husband came home. She knew she was near her confinement, and the question that pressed upon her was "Can I prevent him knowing this, so that I shall not be left a deserted woman?" Having that desire all she states is consistent, - all except the one expression which may to some extent press against her, - all is consistent with the desire -

'[Here the prisoner at the bar was seized with a fit, and had to be carried from the dock. Mr. Couchman, surgeon to the prison, was at once in attendance and, the prisoner was able to reappear in five or six minutes.]

'Mr. Browne: With the exception of one remark, the whole of the statements made were consistent with the very natural desire that her fall from purity should be concealed from her husband, but they show no desire at all, if you can fancy a mother entertaining a desire, of the kind, to destroy her offspring. It is so inconsistent with our knowledge as fathers, and I as a father am addressing you as fathers, it is so inconsistent with our experience to find a mother desirous to destroy her child. Do we not know how she sacrifices too often her health and often her life? Do we not know how to her the care of her infant is as much wrapped up in her existence as if it was the care of her own life? And yet we are to suppose, gentlemen, on the theory of the prosecution, that this woman wilfully and maliciously took away the life of her child. She was a mother before, and a kind mother as we have heard; and we have heard nothing to lead us to suppose that she was not a good wife so long as her husband was with her. It is your duty therefore, to be most thoroughly satisfied that the act was committed by the prisoner not unintentionally, not accidentally, but with malice afore-thought. We have from her statement the fact that she was frightened by a dog previous to her confinement; that she was taken ill very suddenly, as is clear from the stains found first in her lower room and then made before death. Therefore the mark of the collar around the neck would be the same if the collar were put on after as before death. Now as to the question of independent circulation. That is shown by the action of the heart, and it is admitted that this can take place before there is that separate life which you, gentlemen, must find to have existed before you can find that this woman caused its death. You have to find a separate life in the child. It won't do to say the child breathed, that it had circulation, that it respired, that the heart acted, that the lungs acted: all these facts are consistent with non-independent existence, and I cannot find any fact in the medical evidence to justify you in saying, what you must say, before you move a step in this matter, that the child must have lived. My lord will, I have no doubt, go carefully through the medical testimony, but as far as I was able to follow it it amounted to no more than what Dr. Robinson himself said – that the child had respired [breathed]. The learned counsel made a concluding eloquent appeal to the feelings of the jury, leaving the issue in their hands with a conviction that they would give the prisoner the benefit of the doubt which must exist in their minds on the evidence adduced [brought forward].

'His Lordship summed up with much care and legal power, explaining to the jury that it was open to them, in the event of not being convinced of the prisoner's guilt on the capital indictment, to find a verdict of concealment of birth, which the evidence left no doubt of. He expressed the strongest belief that the prisoner had never wished the child should live.

'The Jury immediately returned a verdict of Not Guilty of Wilful Murder, but Guilty of concealment of birth.

'Sentence: 18 calendar months' imprisonment. The prisoner again fainted at this stage, and was borne out of the dock by the warders.'

This leaves the reader wondering what the verdict might be today, and the sentence too.

Sources:

The Bedford Times and Independent, Tuesday March 22, 1870, p.6
Collins English Dictionary

FATAL ACCIDENT IN BEDFORD

William Thomas Poulter

On Saturday March 27, 1897 *The Bedfordshire Times and Independent* reported [page 7] the tragic death of a young boy who was working at the time of the accident which ended his life.

'On Saturday afternoon, at the Infirmary, Dr. Prior (the Borough Coroner) held an enquiry into the circumstances attending the death of a lad, named William Thomas Poulter, who was admitted to the Infirmary on Thursday with serious injuries, and who died on Friday morning. Mr Mark Sharman attended on behalf of deceased's father: – William Poulter, an engineer of 35, Coventry-road, Queen's Park, identified the body as that of his son, who was an errand boy, and who was 14 years old. He was employed by Mr Hauberg, cycle agent, of Midland-road.

'In answer to a question by the Foreman of the Jury (Mr. Rabbitt), witness stated that his son was not deaf. - William Wright, coachman to Mr. W. Mills, of Cardington, stated that on Thursday, March 18, he went to the Midland Station with a horse and dog-cart to buy two papers. He was accompanied by a man named Hobbins. He returned from the station at about 3 p.m., and went by Midland-road. When he got in front of the Grafton Hotel the horse suddenly started, and went left handed on to the pavement. Hobbin was thrown out with the seat, which left witness at the bottom of the cart holding the reins. He remained in that position until the horse fell at the corner of Prebend-street. He shouted for assistance, and a man came and took hold of the horse's head. He got down, and observed that the harness was broken at the hame [a metal bar attached to the horse's collar, with the ropes fastened to them]. He had felt a jerk before the horse started, and had noticed that he could not pull on one side. He produced the near side hame, which was broken off short. It was unsound, and had not been properly welded. He never saw anything of the boy and was not cognisant of any accident until he was out of the cart. He had only had the horse two months; it was not nervous, and he had never known it to shy.

'By Mr. Sharman: He had had the harness twelve months, but had never noticed any defect in it. Charles Hobbins, a helper in Mr. Mills's stables, corroborated the evidence given by the last witness. - George Arthur Sempkins, an auctioneer's clerk, of Westbourne-road, said that on the Thursday in question he was at the corner of Prebend-street. He heard a shout, and, on looking up, saw a horse swerving towards the pavement. As the off wheel caught the kerb, the last witness was thrown from the cart with the seat. Practically at the same moment the hub of the near wheel caught the ladder on which Poulter stood. It was a step ladder, and the lad was about five steps high. The ladder was swept from under him, and he saw the boy fall on his head on the pavement. He was taken into Mr. Stafford's office, and was afterwards removed to the Infirmary in a cab. The horse swerved again into the road until it fell at the corner of Prebend-street. The driver stuck pluckily to the horse, trying to pull it up.

'By Mr Sharman [lawyer]: The driver was quite sober – Mr. S. J. Rose House Surgeon at the Infirmary, stated that the deceased was admitted to the Infirmary at about 4 p.m. on Thursday, suffering from a fracture of the skull and four fractured ribs on the left side, with penetration of the lungs. At one o'clock on Friday morning he suddenly became worse and died shortly afterwards. He made a post mortem examination and found in addition to the above injuries that the stomach was ruptured in two places, a spleen was ruptured, and there was external bruising of both kidneys.

'The Coroner, in summing up, said that it was a relief to him to find that no blame was attachable to anybody. The Driver seemed to have exercised all presence of mind possible. He drew the attention of the Jury to the harness, and he asked all other persons but the Jury to leave the room, as they would reconsider the condition of the harness in private. On returning, the Coroner stated that no blame was attachable to anyone, but great credit was due to the driver for the presence of mind which he showed. - The Jury brought in a verdict of "accidental death" and added a rider to the effect that it was their opinion that the accident was occasioned by the unsound work of the hame, and that such work ought not to have been passed by the foreman of the works where it was made.'

It would seem that the traces, which are the ropes or lengths of leather joined to the hames or bars of metal which in turn attach to the horse's collar on each side, were the cause of the accident. If either of these fractures, the driver is only able to pull on one rein, pulling the horse tightly to one side. In other words, the steering mechanism is disabled. This explains why the horse veered to one side and eventually fell.

A Typical Delivery Cart

As a result of this failure to control the horse, the child suffered four fractured ribs, penetrating the lungs, stomach rupture in two places, a ruptured spleen and external bruising of both kidneys; it would appear to indicate that he had more likely been struck by the horse or the cart. With skull fractures in addition to these injuries, suffered by falling from a ladder onto his head, it was unlikely that the victim could survive, with the limited medical interventions at that time, 1897.

The Education Act of 1870 provided secondary education for children from 5 to 12 years. At that age the vast majority of school leavers joined the workforce and were regarded less as children than young adults [the article refers to William as a 'lad']. On leaving school it was expected that the youngsters would immediately pass into employment. William was employed and working as an 'errand boy' and undertaking a task for his employer which window cleaners today might well consider risky on a busy day in Midland Road or Prebend Street, balanced precariously on a ladder. Such was the life of working-class children.

Prebend Street, little changed today.

William Thomas Poulter came from a large family, living at the time of the accident at 35 Coventry Road, Queens Park. The 1891 Census shows that William Poulter (senior) was living at 59 Carpenter Street, Battersea, describing himself as an engineer borer; the facts tend to indicate that he was employed by the WH Allen York Street Works in Lambeth, situated alongside Waterloo Station. He was living on a direct railway line to the Allen works. The expanding Waterloo Station was responsible for the relocation of the Allen works c. 1890 and their establishment in Bedford. William Poulter, his wife Elizabeth and family are believed to be one of the hundred or so Allen workforce who themselves relocated to Bedford. The 1895 Bedford Directory shows the family living in an unnumbered newly-built house [October 1894] along with two engineer neighbours, a vacant house, one occupied by a professor of music, a fifth occupied by a coal merchant and with a further house under construction. These were the early days of development in Queens Park. The development was first proposed in 1887, in the run-up to Queen Victoria's Jubilee that year, which is why the area was named Queen's Park, and Allen's was known as Queen's Engineering Works. William Poulter maintained his position in the company and was 'superannuated' for his services, and loyalty perhaps. William Henry Allen, the founder, died in 1926 and the company finally closed down c. 2000.

The company sustained William and Elizabeth and their large family. In the 1901 Census William is described as an engine maker, aged 48. Living with him was his wife Elizabeth, three daughters and seven sons. William Thomas had been their second child, so eleven children at least. Their daughters Elizabeth and Emily were laundry workers, Walter aged 14 was a baker's boy, five children were at school, one was aged two and one younger. The 1911 Census shows they had moved to 5 Westbourne Road,

Queen's Park. William was aged 58 and Elizabeth his wife aged 50. The eldest of the children is R Samuel Poulter aged 22, an electrical engineer, one son is a moulder, two are errand boys, one in a dairy. There is a grandson aged 8, so eight children and a grandson. This was an industrious family with a good work ethic, sustained largely by their income from Allens.

Workers at the W H Allen works at York Street c. 1890, courtesy M. Nicholson.

It is a sad fact that William Thomas Poulter lost his life whilst working to help support his many siblings. The owner of the horse and cart and the drivers of that vehicle were perhaps not as safety-conscious as they could have been; they had to tack-up every day before venturing out with the horse and cart and it is perhaps surprising that they did not notice a weakness in the harness which they were handling and should have been inspecting. It was tragic that William Thomas lost his life as a result of this, but had the horse bolted there may well have been further fatalities, and it is likely the driver of the vehicle would have lost his life also.

William Thomas Poulter's father, William Poulter, died in the first quarter of 1917 and his wife died in the last quarter of 1923. The Bedford Directory for 1918 shows that Elizabeth Poulter is the main householder living at 5 Westbourne Road. The Bedford Directory for 1925 shows William Thomas's brother Charles Poulter [born 11.06.1890] as the main householder, described as a Moulder – possibly still working at Allens. He later moved to 25 Oldfield Road [1940]; described as a Machine Miller and was married to Alice Jane. His first wife, Agnes, whom he married in 1913, died in 1916. He joined The Royal Engineers in 1914 [Territorial Force] according to the British Army Service Records, and was living in Brighton on 25 April 1914 [WW1 Pension Records]. Charles Poulter was discharged from the Royal Engineers unfit for military service, 8 August 1914.

Charles Lipscombe Poulter may have been unfit for millitary service, but according to *The Bedfordshire Times and Independent,* March 9 1934 p. 15 and *The Bedfordshire Mercury October* 5 1906 he was a football referee [1934] registered with The Bedfordshire FA and was still refereeing in 1939. He died in 1960.

William Thomas Poulter would have been proud of his brother I believe. He himself was less fortunate, dying at such a young age. He was buried in an unmarked grave at Bedford Cemetery on March 25 1897.

Sources:

1895, 1918, 1925 Bedford Directory
1891, 1901 and 1911 Census
The British Army Service Records
WW1 Pension Records
The Bedfordshire Times and Independent Saturday March 27 1897 p. 7
Bedfordshire Mercury October 5 1906
Bedfordshire Times and Independent March 9 1934 p.15
The Allen Magazine, York Street Works October 1950
Grave Plan G5, Section 192

Photographs:

Allen workers c.1890 – The Allen Magazine, York Street Works October 1950
Mr M Boyles (Bedfordshire's Yesteryears)
Grave site Ref. G5 192
Prebend Street Maurice Nicholson (origin unknown)

SAD CASE OF DROWNING IN THE RIVER OUSE

Cecil Talbot Read

It is not surprising to hear of yet another drowning in the River Ouse in Bedford, but this one is rather different to the many we have encountered so far, but the outcome was the same in all cases, the loss of a precious life.

'An inquest was held at the Ship Inn, St. Cuthbert's, on Tuesday morning, before Mr. Mark Whyley, Deputy Coroner, on the body of Cecil Talbot Read, son of Capt. Read, Park-road, who was drowned in the Ouse by the upsetting of a sailing-boat the previous day. The following gentlemen were sworn on the jury: Messrs. T. Hague (foreman), P. W. Barker, E. Peacock, G. Mallows, F. Fuller, Q. Harris, S. Groom, M. Mountane, J. Jefferies, R. Richards, J. C. Revis, G. Barnes, and W. Coote.

'Constantine Heywood Read deposed [witnessed in court]: I am the father of the deceased. He was 18 years of age on the 13th of last February. It is the body of my son which the jury have viewed this morning. He was in the merchant service and had served five years in the ship P. F. Webster. He had been voyaging for the past 5 years. He could not swim. I last saw him alive when he left home at half-past one. He did not say where he was going, but I understood that he was going to Kempston, fishing with his brother. I next heard of him at a quarter past four from Mr. Baxter. I and my wife were going to post some letters, when Mr. Baxter told me that he had been drowned and was being taken to the mortuary. I went to the mortuary and identified the body of my son; it was quite warm.

'Alfred Ernest Anthony, architect and surveyor, deposed: Yesterday afternoon just after half-past two I was passing along the bottom part of the embankment going in the direction of High-street, when I saw the lad put out in a boat from Chetham's place. It was a lug-sailed [square-sail] boat with centre board. He went across the river alright. I made a remark to one of Chetham's men that he did not seem to know very much about boat-sailing. He went once across the river and then put her before the wind, which was due west and very gusty. He had not gone above 30 or 40 yards before the wind struck the sail which jibbed over, and the boat running up into the wind went broadside on and eventually turned right over on her side, and gradually filling with water, sank. The evident cause of the accident was that he either had the sheet fastened or entangled in such a way that he could not let it free. In my Opinion if he could have got the sheet free, she would have righted herself. While I was watching him I saw a boat containing three persons scull straight by the poor fellow. The end of their sculls [small oars, used with one hand] were within three yards (or five yards at the outside) of deceased and they might easily have thrown one to him.

'Capt. Read: And might have saved him!

'Witness, continuing: These people are strangers to the town. Perhaps they were paralysed with fear and dared not go near him.

'The Coroner: They were strangers to you?

'Witness: Yes. They were strangers to the town from what I can gather. I think the least they should have done was to throw him a scull. On seeing they went past I immediately ran down the embankment, took off my coat and waistcoat, and jumped into the river. As I jumped in I could see that he was then evidently done for. He was fighting with the water as hard as he could. He soon exhausted himself, and when I was 10 yards from the bank he went down. I knew it was useless to proceed any further. Someone came up with a boat, and two men undressed and dived for him. I sent to Goatley's for the drags and we commenced dragging. Insp. Haynes first found the body, but owing to the shifting of the boat he dropped. I was the first to take hold of the body and we landed it on the bank. We commenced dragging at 23 minutes to three and it was close on four o'clock before we found the body. Where we found it the water was 14 or 15 feet deep.

'In reply to a Juryman the witness said the party who passed by hired their boat from Goatley's.

'The Foreman: It was very great cowardice on their part.

'Witness said there was a midshipman with the party.

'Inspector Haynes deposed: just after three yesterday afternoon I received information that there was a body in the river. I procured the drags and immediately commenced dragging for it. After dragging some time I hooked the body and brought it to the surface, but the man who was sculling me suddenly jumped up from his seat and rushed to the side of the boat. No doubt he thought he could assist me. There was a danger of our being capsized and the body got loose from the drag and sank again. After dragging a little longer Mr. Anthony hooked it. I got into his boat and took it in charge, landing it at Chetham's on the Embankment side. I then searched the body and found on it the watch and chain which I produce. It had stopped at 21 minutes to three. I also found two tobacco pouches, a key, pencil, a match box, 4s. 9d. in silver, and 7d in coppers. I then put the body straight and had it conveyed to the mortuary. I knew the deceased. I had spoken to him several times.

'The Coroner asked the inspector if he had instructions to take all bodies found in the river to the mortuary, whether they were known or unknown.

'Inspector Haynes said if bodies were found in the river they were taken to the mortuary. The coroner had power to order their removal home.

'In reply to the foreman, the witness said he did not know where the party in the boat came from. One was a midshipman and another member of the party was a man as tall as himself (the inspector) and stouter. They were pointed out to him in the street.

'A juryman: Did you ask them any questions?

'Inspector Haynes: No I did not. I had no power.

'Frank Smith deposed: I am a waterman in the employ of Mr. Chetham and am stationed by the Embankment. I know the deceased. He had several times hired boats off me. He came down about half-past twelve yesterday, but the boat was then out and he said he should like to have it after dinner. He came again at half-past two and started by himself. He had several times been out in the boat. It was a 12 feet boat with a centre board of iron.

It also had iron ballast. It was shaped ballast.

'The Coroner: Under the floor boards or not?

'Witness: Yes

'The Coroner: Was it made fast?

'Witness: No it was loose.

'The Coroner: Did you see it when the boat started away?

'Witness: Yes

'The Coroner: Whereabouts was it?

'Witness: In the bows of the boat.

'The Coroner: How many pieces of ballast were there?

'Witness: One; it weighed about 56lbs.

'Mr Anthony said the ballast weighed exactly 48lbs.

'Witness: I did not watch him because I had to start a boat at another part of the Embankment. I left a man in my place. I saw him in the water and rowed towards him as hard as I could. I pulled off my coat and dived after him. I went to the bottom four or five times. I kept on as long as I could, but could find nothing of him. I asked him before he went out whether I should reef the sail. He said "Not for this lot of wind." I said "I suppose you are not like some. I suppose you can swim?" He replied, "Swim, I should think I can." I did not notice whether he made the sheet fast by the side of the boat.

'The foreman: You do not know the people that passed?

'Witness: No

'The foreman: You saw them go by?

'Witness: Yes; I saw them as they rowed away to the Embankment.

'The foreman: It is a great pity we don't know who they are.

'Mr. G. Robinson, surgeon, deposed to being called by the police a few minutes after four to see the deceased. He met the body being carried to the mortuary, where he afterwards examined it. The body itself was warm, but the extremities were cold. There was not the slightest pulsation or sign of life. Death must have taken place more than an hour from the coldness of the extremities. There were no marks of violence, and all appearances went to show that drowning was the cause of death.

'The Coroner, in summing up, said the evidence showed conclusively what was the cause of death, and they had heard sufficient to give a satisfactory verdict as to that. Then the question arose as to the inhumanity and dastardly conduct of those people who went by and did not render assistance. But even if they knew them and they were brought there they had no means of punishing them, and all they could do was to express their indignation at, and their thorough detestation of such conduct.

'This met with the unanimous approval of the jury, and the foreman said they felt very strongly about the matter: the men in the boat had acted in a very cowardly manner. He commended the conduct of Smith for endeavouring to find deceased.

'The Coroner said the next point was whether the deceased had sufficient knowledge to be entrusted with a boat of that description. The evidence, however, on that point went to show that he had been out in the boat several times, but although he had been 5 years in the merchant service, yet it was possible that he had no idea of the danger he was running in a sailing boat. They would observe that he asked the Inspector what his instructions were as to the removal of the bodies found in the river (whether they were known or unknown) to the mortuary. He asked the question in no captious [frivolous or vexatious objections ie annoying or disappointing] spirit, but he thought if a person was known to live in the town it added to the misery and pain of the relatives if he were taken to the mortuary instead of being taken home. In this case there was no reason for taking the body there; there was no question as to the cause of death; the only question was whether any one was to blame.

'A juryman thought it would be too great a shock to the relatives to take the body home at once.

'The Coroner said the police might notify the fact beforehand.

'The jury returned a verdict of "Accidentally Drowned," and complimented Inspector Haynes and the others who were engaged in the prompt search for the body.'

According to the 1881 census, the family lived at 6 Park Road [now Glebe Road]. Cecil's father was Captain Constantine Hayward Read aged 54. a retired officer late of the Ceylon Rifles. He was born 16 September 1826 and died at Bedford 12 February 1888. Also living there were Caroline Read his wife aged 52, a son aged 22, an undergraduate, and Sarah aged 16, a servant. There is no mention of Cecil but it is obvious from the inquest document that he was at home on the day in question, having left at 'half past one.' Cecil was 18 and it seems he began work in the merchant navy aged 13. Although not regarded as a child at eighteen, either then nor now, his sad demise is recorded here as it illustrates just how easy it was to fall prey to the river even though he indicated that he could swim. Younger children had no chance of surviving should they fall into the river, and woefully this occurred quite regularly. The 'drags' used to recover bodies must have been a common sight on the Ouse.

Sad to say, William Wood Dewes, Cecil's brother, died off Cape Finisterre whilst homeward bound, on 17 May 1882 aged 21 years. Cecil died on 21 August 1882 aged 18. Their mother Caroline Read died in 1903.

Sources:

The Bedfordshire Times and Independent, Saturday, 26 August, 1882 p.6
1881 Census
Died c. 21 August 1882 aged 18Buried in Bedford Cemetery 24 August 1882
Grave ref. G5 132 address recorded as 6 Park Road (now Glebe Road), St Peters

MELANCHOLY DEATH IN ELSTOW

Fanny Woods

The following item appeared in the local press on Saturday, 4 September 1880:

'On Saturday morning last a melancholy death took place at Medbury Farm, Elstow, which is in the occupation of Mr. J. L. Prole. The deceased was a servant girl named Fanny Woods, and was only 17 years of age. The circumstances attending the death will be found in the evidence below, which was taken at the inquest held by Mr. Wiseman, deputy coroner for the Queen's honour of Ampthill, at the farm house, on Monday afternoon. The following were sworn on the jury: - William Henry Lardeaux (foreman), Joseph Smith, Robert James, William Southam, Thomas Bowler, John Watford, William Warden, James Litchfield, Edward Kind, William Chamberlain, William Crouch, Joseph Harper, William Sharp, and William Desborough.

'Ann Woods, wife of Am. Woods, labourer, Bletsoe, said: The deceased was my daughter, and was 17 years of age last March. She went out as a domestic servant, and was in service with Mrs. Woodger, Bedford, a fortnight, previously to coming to Mr. Prole's. She was at home at Michaelmas last, but I did not suspect anything then. I also saw her two months ago, and then I suspected she was pregnant, but she utterly denied it. I have not seen her alive since. I saw her on Saturday at Mr. Prole's, and she was dead. My daughter came to Mr. Prole's the latter end of April. In November last she was in service at Mr. Hine's at Knotting for a month, coming away the beginning of December.

'Mr. Joseph Lilley Prole said: I am a farmer at Medbury Farm, and the deceased was in my service. She came in April last as kitchenmaid. Whilst she has been here she had no followers [romantic associations?], and conducted herself very quietly. I had not the slightest suspicion that she was enciente [pregnant], and never heard anything from any of the household. On Saturday morning last, at about 7.30, I saw the deceased in the yard. She had a pail in her left hand, and her right arm was covered with blood. I saw her go into the closet, and I went into the back kitchen and saw a lot of blood about. I watched the closet for about 10 minutes, and as she did not come out I called my wife, telling her that I thought something was the matter, and she had better go. She went to the closet and returned in two or three minutes, and from what she told me I said, "something must be done." I went out into a field close by and returned in about ten minutes, and my wife told me the deceased had not returned. We sent for a woman, and she went to her but we had to call some men, and I went with them to the closet. We found the girl on the floor, and she was carried upstairs. We gave her some tea and whisky, and sent for the doctor, and he arrived soon afterwards, but she was dead then. I found a new-born child dead in the closet on Sunday about midday. We had examined the closet the previous day, but did not succeed in finding it. In fact it was not until after a post mortem examination had been made of the deceased, and from what the doctor said, that we were certain she had been confined, so I then made a more thorough examination.

'Dr. J. Coombs, in practice at Bedford, said: I have seen the deceased occasionally at the farm, but never suspected she was pregnant. She was a girl of unusual size, very fat. On Saturday morning, about 3 o'clock, Mr. Edward Prole, brother of the last witness, came to fetch me, and I started with him immediately. I found the deceased lying on the bed where she had been placed, she was quite dead – and had been dead about half-an-hour. I made an examination of the body and ascertained that she had either miscarried or had given birth to a child. Yesterday (Sunday) morning I made a post mortem examination of the body with the assistance of my son, Mr. R. H. Coombs, and was satisfied that the deceased had given birth to a child. It was then that Mr. Prole made a closer examination of the closet and I saw the child brought out. It was a full-grown male child. There were no marks of violence or injury on the child. The deceased died from haemorrhage consequent on parturition.

'This was the whole of the evidence, and the jury having consulted together for a short time, they unanimously gave a verdict in accordance with the medical testimony.'

Poor girl, abandoned to suffer alone at a young age, and remain in employment throughout the pregnancy and birth. Did anyone consider who might be responsible in such cases? Whatever the circumstances someone should have taken responsibility and offered her and her baby support. A melancholy death indeed for a terrified mother and an innocent baby boy.

Source:

The Bedfordshire Times and Independent, 4 September 1880 p.8

FATAL ACCIDENT AT THE REGATTA

Caroline Ridge

The Bedford Regatta was and still is, the major local event of the year. It attracts many people locally and from further afield to participate or just to enjoy the colourful activities taking place all along the river in the centre of town. One such event in 1869 took a more dramatic turn, with terrible consequences, as recorded in the local Press:

'We regret to have to record that a fatal accident has attended this year's Regatta. At about half-past eight a little girl named Caroline Ridge, [Diana Caroline Ridge] aged 10, ran in front of the gun with which the boats were started just as it was being fired, and received such serious injuries to the upper part of her neck, which was much lacerated, that she died within an hour and a half after being taken to the General Infirmary. The cannon was at the time in charge of Sergeant Ashley Hartley, of the 82nd Regiment, now in Bedford on recruiting service. He was apprehended almost directly after, but was bailed on being taken before a magistrate. On Friday morning he appeared before Mr. Alderman Trapp and Captain Jackson, on the charge of feloniously killing and slaying the girl, but formal evidence, for the purpose of a remand, having been taken, the further hearing of the charge was postponed to Monday, the 19th. Sergeant

Hartley was admitted to bail in £25 and one surety in the same sum.'

The Inquest

'On Saturday evening, the 17th inst., an inquest was held at the General Infirmary by Dr. Prior, borough coroner, on the body of Caroline Ridge (aged 10), daughter of Mr. [George] Ridge, The Albion, Harpur-street. The death of this unfortunate little girl has been already noticed in connexion with our report of the regatta, but the full particulars will be found in the subjoined report of the evidence taken by the Coroner.

'The following were empanelled as the Jury. - Mr. P. S. Fry, foreman; Messrs. John Andrews, John Hardwick, Charles Albert Reeves, Thomas Bull, Benjamin Harrison, Wm. Samuels, Isaac Simpkin, Edward Smith, James Pratt, William Webbs, Thomas Harding, and Thomas Stock.

'Mr. L. Jessopp, solicitor, appeared to watch the proceedings on behalf of Sergeant Ashley Hartley, 82nd Infantry Regiment. The body having been viewed, the following witnesses were examined:-

'Thomas Pearson: I am an upholsterer and reside in Castle-lane. On Thursday last I was engaged by the Regatta Committee, to start the boats, just below Waterloo. [Waterloo being a row of dilapidated cottages which stood on the embankment, situated roughly opposite the War Memorial. These properties have been demolished and the ground laid to lawn and gardens]. My boat was moored opposite the locks. Two small cannons were placed on a block on the embankment, but previous to the accident the man who had charge of them in the morning, and who fired one or other of them all the day, had dismounted one of them. Just as the boats had started the cannons were fired in order to let the public know that the race had commenced. About 8 o'clock, p.m., I was sitting in my boat, just as a race was about to start. At this time one of the cannons had been dismounted, Sergeant Dyer, who had charge of them having said he would fire no more cannons. Just as the race was about to start it was my place to lay hold of one of the boats until the umpire gave the word "Go!" after having twice asked "Are you ready?" At this time a four-oared race was started, and just as the boat left my hand the cannon was fired. My head being turned in the direction of the cannon, I saw the deceased child fall immediately the discharge took place. The child's head fell into the river. I pulled my boat across as quickly as possible, thinking the child was my niece, and I said "Who will fetch the doctor?" as I saw that the child had been shot. Sergeant Hartley was standing by and I said to him "You have killed the child." He was against where the child was, and I had seen fire the cannon. He said "It's done!" I then walked down the embankment and saw a policeman, to whom I said, "There is a child shot and Sergeant Hartley has done it. He has just gone out of the baulk" [a thick beam].

'By the Foreman: The cannon might be two yards from the river edge. Just in front of it there was a little bit of a nook, about three yards, and the child must have run around by that in order to get to the front of the cannon, unless, of course, the child had been standing there previously. A lot of people stood there. The cannon was placed sideways so as to shoot off the river rather slanting, and thereby to avoid the people.

Riverbank by Waterloo

'By Mr. Bull: The elevation of the gun was rather over Mr Harrison's mill (something about 45 degrees).

'By the Foreman: There were a great many children and grown-up people about the cannon, but I could not see any in front of it. When the gun was about to be fired in the fore-part of the day I heard the word given to "Clear the way!" The poor child must have been in front of the cannon; she was standing there, for as I lay I could not help seeing the cannon. I did not see her run in front of it, but I should think there were a score others standing about it, and they were all on the move.

'To the Coroner: I did not hear "Clear the way" in the latter part of the day.

'A Juror: This little grip was originally Mr. Rogers' boat-house.

'By a Juror: On this occasion the cannon was fired as soon as the boats were started

'Another Juror: Can you state a reason?

'Witness: According to my own judgment I can give a reason. The man who had charge of the cannon in the forepart of the day got drunk, and he was incapable of taking charge of it after.

'By Mr. Bull: I had hardly let the boat out of my hand when the cannon was fired.

'The Coroner: Mr. Bull can state what were the instructions given by the committee.

'Mr. T. Bull: Early in the morning I went down to Mr. Dyer, and gave him instructions in my capacity of member of the Regatta Committee. Those instructions were - that when the umpire gave the final word "Are you ready, gentlemen?" - "Go!" the cannon was not to be fired at that moment, but that the boats should be allowed to proceed a short distance, say up to the locks, before the gun should be fired to warn boats off the course and give the public information that the race had commenced.

'The witness Pearson (to a Juror): I should think that the elevation of the gun was such that, at the distance of two yards in front of it, the explosion would touch anybody of any size.

'A Juror: Why was it removed this year from Mr Harrison's meadow?

'Mr. Harrison: Because I would not allow it.

'By Mr. Hardwick: Sergeant Dyer, of the Beds. Militia, had charge of the cannon in the morning. Two races went off for which he could not fire the cannon at all. He became incapable from drunkenness of firing the gun at all during the latter part of the day. That is to say, I am speaking as far as my judgment will allow, for if I saw a man acting like him I should say he was not capable.

'A Juror: Could the person in charge of the cannon see the child in front of it?

'Witness: Could I see you, sir?

'The Juror: You could if you look.

'Witness: So could he see the child?

'Mr. Harrison: Had the gun been properly elevated the explosion would have gone over the head of the person two yards in front of the muzzle.

'By the Juror: Sergeant Hartley was with Dyer during some parts of the afternoon. I did not see Sergeant Hartley the worse for liquor in any way.

'By Mr. Bull: I could not swear that the child was standing in front of the cannon when the fuse was applied. [We may here state that the gun was fired by means of an ordinary cigar fusee (a kind of match), instead of a fuse.]

'Daniel James Hostler deposed: I am a labourer working at Messrs. Howards'. At about 8 p.m. I was sitting on the bank near the starting-place, with my wife and niece. Immediately the two four-oars race started I looked towards the cannons so that I might caution my wife as to the report. I saw Sergeant Hartley strike the fusee and put it to the touch hole. The cannon went off, and the child, who was standing in front of the cannon, dropped. She was standing near Sergeant Dyer in front of the cannon, just before it was fired. I did not notice her until a minute or two before the boats started, for my attention was just then drawn to Sergeant Dyer, by something he said to one of the crews.

'To the Foreman: The child was standing on the little bit of a grip.

'To Jurors: When I saw the child she was standing close to Sergeant Dyer, but I did not see that he had hold of her hand. I was rather askew to the cannon; I should think about eight or nine yards from it.

'By Mr Harrison: I saw the child move about before the cannon was fired. I think she was talking to Sergeant Dyer. She didn't make a sudden bolt to the front of the cannon.

'To Mr. Jessopp: The cannon was elevated at about 45 degrees, and stood about 18 inches from the ground.

'Witness (to the Coroner or the Jurors): Sergeant Dyer did not give the order to clear the way while I was there. The boats had gone about 50 yards when the cannon was fired, and I should think the child was about 3 yards in front of it. In the early part of the day I heard the order to clear the way. I heard Sergeant Dyer say something to one of the crews, but could not tell what. I could not say that Sergeant Dyer was sober. I had seen him come to the public-house two or three times in the afternoon.

'The Coroner: He might go to the public-house and not be drunk necessarily.

'Witness: His actions showed he was not sober. If he was sober I am not sober now. He seemed quite lost, and did not know what he was doing.

'Mr Harrison: In what state was the man who fired the

cannon?

'Witness: He had had beer; anyone could tell that. He had been in company with Sergeant Dyer. I was down there three times in the afternoon and saw them drinking together. In my opinion he was not so drunk as Dyer.

'The Foreman: If he was not sober then, how could he have been sober in five minutes?

'Witness: Well, sir, the fright might take great effect upon him.

'The Juror: The man was staggering about, was he not?

'The Coroner: Was he making a noise or abusive?

'Witness: No. Sergeant Dyer was foolish. He could scarcely stand at all. Sergeant Hartley walked as well as he could I believe.

'The Coroner: I know of my own knowledge that he is crippled at present.

'By Mr. Bull: If the man were lame that would account for the way he walked.

'By a Juror: I must say there was a great difference between Sergeant Dyer and the other.

'To the Coroner: I cannot say that Sergeant Hartley was the worse for liquor.

'To Mr. Jessopp: I should think the child was standing three yards from the cannon when it was fired. Dyer seemed to stand at the corner of the grip, side-ways from the child. Sergeant Quarry was standing near the cannon and close to the side of the child when the cannon was fired, and I should think it must have almost blown him over.

'William Guest deposed: I am a smith and work at Mr. Kilpin's. I was on the embankment close to the cannon, and a great many people were around. I heard no order to clear the way. When the boats started I ran along the bank, and when I had gone about ten or twenty steps the cannon was fired. I then heard the cry that someone was shot, and as I had lost my little girl, who was with me a minute or two before, I turned back. I turned up the face of the child, and saw it was not my own girl. I then gave all the assistance in my power. There was plenty of room for anyone to pass between the cannon and the river.

'Mr. Jessopp: Was Dyer drunk?

'Witness: I cannot say. My opinion was that he had a little beer, but he was not thrown off his guard or anything of the sort.

'Mr. Jessop: Then he was not drunk?

'Witness: Oh dear, no! He could stand upright as well as I could. Sergeant Dyer was not incapable. He asked me for a fusee or lucifer and I found two or three. I handed them to him and he said "That's the boy." That occurred previous to the fatal shot, by about two or three minutes.

'To a Juror: Sergeant Dyer seemed excited. I know nothing of Sergeant Hartley.

'At this stage one of the Jurors stated that Sergeant Dyer should be called, and a policeman was sent for him. Sergeant Dyer was soon in attendance, but it was decided not to call him.

'Sergeant James Quarry, Militia Staff: I was so near the cannon when it was fired that the nap of my neck was singed. Having never been at a regatta before I thought the boats were started by firing of the gun, and having seen the boats started I naturally went close to the river. Thinking that the cannon had yet to be fired off. The child must have been close to me, in fact touching me, for when the cannon was fired I knew I was struck somewhere, and at first I thought that my coat tails had been taken off. The moment the gun was fired I saw the little girl swept to the water, and her head got in. I think no one else saw her fall but myself, for nobody offered to pick her up, all being intent on looking at the boats. Shortly after the accident a lad from the country, whom I do not know, told me that Sergeant Hartley called out to clear the way and that he pulled him back from the front of the gun. Sergeant Dyer must have been looking at the race as well as I. I really believe nobody could have told who fired the cannon if Sergeant Hartley had not owned it at once himself. I heard Sergeant Dyer enquire immediately who had fired the gun.

'To the Foreman: Sergeant Hartley was sober, I believe.

'To a Juror: I didn't take notice of Sergeant Dyer. He seemed to be sober. As a military man I   should not have taken the position I did had I known that the cannon was about to be fired. Had they called out "clear the way" I should, if I had looked, have taken particular care to leave the way. Powder exploded in that manner has a tendency to lateral expansion. I thought the gun was not sufficiently elevated, considering that the people were round it. It would have been right enough if the people did not crowd around it. Sergeant Hartley was taken into custody.

'A Juror suggested that in this event, the policeman who took Hartley into custody could speak to his sobriety. Sergeant Hartley was, accordingly, requested to retire. In his absence

Police-constable Edward Wm. Walford deposed: About eight o'clock the witness Pearson called me to fetch Sergeant Hartley back as he had shot a child. The sergeant was then walking steadily up the baulk. Directly I overtook him he said "I know what you have come for. I own I let the cannon off. Is the child dead? I hope in God she is not." He was perfectly sober.

'Police-constable Wm. Henry Haynes (the inquest officer) stated that he entered the charge against Hartley at the station, and that Hartley was then perfectly sober, and had lodged for two years at the house of the child's father.

'Sergeant Ashley Hartley then voluntarily gave the following evidence: Between 7 and 8 o'clock Dyer asked me if I would fire the cannon, and gave me a pipe fusee and a piece of stick to which I attached the fusee. He told me I was to fire as soon as the boats had started. Previous to firing I told the people to clear the way in front and to get to one side. I saw the front cleared, and then lit the fusee, but it dropped out of the stick. I picked it up and lit it again, and then applied it to the touch-hole with my hand. Before the fusee dropped the front was clear, but there were people to the right and left. Being in a stooping position at the moment, I could not see that any one was in front, the cannon being pointed in an echelon (askew) direction.

'By Mr. Bull: The elevation of the gun was about 45 degrees, and I should not have thought that it would hit a child at the distance of two or three yards. Had I seen any person even five or six yards in front I should have cautioned them, but still they would be in no danger.

'Wm. Billing, Volunteer sergeant: About nine o'clock on the

same evening I saw Sergeant Dyer at the house of deceased's father, and heard him say that he gave Sergeant Hartley leave to fire off the gun.

'By Juror: Dyer was hardly sober at the time.

'Mr. W. G. Johnson, house Surgeon, Infirmary, deposed that the deceased was received about 8.40 p.m., in an insensible condition, suffering from a lacerated wound about an inch below the occipital protuberance. She never regained consciousness and died within an hour and a half. The Post Mortem examination showed a fracture of the scull and injury of the brain, to which death was attributable.

'After private deliberation the Jury returned a verdict of accidental death, with the following addendum:- "The Jury express a hope that for the future care will be taken by the authorities connected with the river regatta, that the cannons may either be enclosed or placed in such a position that the public cannot be endangered; and also wish to censure Sergeant Dyer for neglect of duty in delegating firing of the cannon to any other person."

'During the enquiry the learned Coroner gave the necessary order that the friends of the deceased should have the body for interment.'

Magisterial Investigation

'On Monday, the 19th inst., at the Borough Petty Sessions, Sergeant Hartley surrendered to his bail on remand from Friday, 16th, on the charge of feloniously killing and slaying Caroline

Ridge. The evidence already taken for the prosecution was read over and did not differ materially from that given at the inquest.

'Wm. Wheatley, fishmonger, Castle-lane, was the only witness then examined who was not called before the Coroner. He deposed on Friday that he had been employed to fetch the cannons home and went about 7.30. The boats had gone about 30 yards, when the cannons went off, and the witness had nearly been blown into the water. He heard no warning given and did not see the child. Could not say there was no warning given.

'Mr Jessopp appeared for the defendant, and the usual form of caution having been gone through, addressed the Bench on the facts brought out in the evidence. He then called

'Frederick Richards (9), a scholar at Mr Riley's school, who deposed as follows: "On the evening of the regatta I was standing by the side of the deceased just before the accident. She ran away from my side just before the cannon was fired, and as she ran away from me I saw her knocked down. I was frightened and ran away. She was only two or three yards from the cannon when she commenced to run.

'To Mr. Burch: I heard Sergeant Hartley make the remark "Are you all clear?" (applause).

'[The manner in which this boy was procured as a witness was rather strange. Mr. Jessopp was inspecting the site of the accident on Sunday evening, when a person standing by pointed out wrongly the position in which the cannon had been placed. This little boy was close to the spot with his aunt, and then described to Mr. Jessopp the entire of the facts as given in his evidence. Before he was called the Chairman (Mr. Howard) asked Mr.

Jessopp could he not bring some one of mature years to give evidence. Mr. Jessopp made an eloquent reply, declaring that the evidence of such a boy was infinitely more creditable than that of adults who might be biassed, and the feeling of the audience was so far enlisted by the remark that they attempted to applaud.]

'The Bench, after nearly two hours and a half had been devoted to the case, conferred together for a few moments.

'The Chairman, in discharging the accused, delivered the following admonition: I need not tell you that this inquiry has been conducted with great deliberation, and very great pains have been taken to ascertain the truth. I could not say that the Bench are thoroughly satisfied that you were as careful as you ought to have been in discharging a deadly weapon but I am glad to tell you there is no disposition to carry this matter any further. We don't feel that the evidence has been sufficient to sustain a charge of manslaughter, but I hope you will take a word of advice from an old man, and that this will be a subject of deep regret to you. If you are a man of any pity, or capable of keen sympathy for the parents of this child, I hope it will be a matter of regret that you, in an unguarded moment and without sufficient caution, have been the instrument of sending a child into another world without a moment's warning. Whenever you are discharging a deadly instrument again be sure you never do so without seeing, at least, that there is no one in front of it.

'Sergeant Hartley (for whom much sympathy was shown, and who evidently has been sadly put about by the unhappy accident) was loudly applauded on leaving the court.'

The Regatta event has taken place in Bedford on the River Ouse for a great many years [since 1853] and there may well have been accidents and even fatalities on various such occasions. It is astonishing to learn that a child was shot through the neck by a cannon, operated by professionals, back in 1869 and that cannons continued to be used during subsequent regattas.

More information about the Regatta, Caroline and her family is to follow.

An artist's impression of Waterloo Cottages.

Waterloo Cottages c. 1891

Clearance of Waterloo for gardens

Sources:

The Bedford Times and Bedfordshire Independent, Tuesday July 20, 1869 p.5

Photographs:

Courtesy M. Nicholson (source unknown)
Butcher's Row courtesy M Nicholson
The Old Water Bridge by the Author

FATAL ACCIDENT AT THE REGATTA (cont.)

Caroline Ridge

Press reports offer a more lucid description of the Regatta, and this leads to more background information of Caroline's family:

Bedford Regatta

'On Thursday last this pleasant annual meeting came off, with a degree of success, which fully corresponded with the anticipations entertained even by the most sanguine of its promoters. The facilities afforded by the Midland and the London and North-Western Railway Companies had the effect of inducing numbers of excursionists to visit the town, the additional attraction of fine weather being also much in favour of the Regatta. Special trains conveyed holiday-makers from Leicester, Northampton, Hitchin, Luton, St Pancras Station and from most of the lesser towns along the lines of the railway, so that the sudden influx of visitors gave a decidedly animated appearance to the principal streets of Bedford.

'By noon there was gathered along the river the largest assemblage we have witnessed for years. The gardens of the Swan Hotel, kindly thrown open by Mr. Wicks for the accommodation of the subscribers to the Regatta fund, affording a delightful promenade during the day to the many who availed themselves of the privilege. The grounds abutting on the portion of the course between the Grammar School and the Britannia Works were occupied by a vast concourse. On the north side Mr. H. A. Dale, of the Kings Arms Inn, had a series of spacious marquees in a pleasant meadow, and we need scarcely add that the spirited caterer was thoroughly attentive to the wants of his numerous patrons. On the opposite bank similar arrangements were made by Mr. J. Napier, of the Star Inn, Harpur-street, who also had a large share of the public patronage. Mr. Smith, who had the letting of the fields, took every precaution to insure the safety of the visitors, and we noticed that on this occasion there was a strong line of hurdles laid along the bank in addition to the usual fencing, the whole being arranged so as to afford protection without interfering with the view of the river. The bridge afforded a vantage position to crowds of spectators, and all along the new embankment there were hundreds gathered during the day. A variety of amusements were provided in the meadows, and the band of the Luton Volunteer Corps was in attendance.

'The arrangements made by the committee were of a satisfactory character, everything having been done to keep down the expenses to a degree consistent with efficiency. The gentlemen on whom this important duty devolved were:- Mr. H. D. Hinrich (chairman of the committee), Rev. F. Fanshawe, Rev. J. Y. Segrave, Messrs. A. E. Burch, W. J. Nash, G. P. Nash, John Sergeant, E. Green, T. Bull, J. B. Lee, and C. E. B. Gillions (Hon. Sec.).

'The course was from a white flag below the locks to a flag near the Midland Railway bridge. The umpires were:- Mr. J. G.

Wood, Emmanuel College, Cambridge, and Mr. E. D. Brickwood, London. They were rowed about for the greater part of the day by Bedford crews. The duties of Judge were performed by Sergeant Major Neat, with the Beds Militia permanent staff.

'The Regatta commenced at Noon, and from the following report it will be seen that clubs from a distance, metropolitan and provincial, were well represented.'

The article gave details of the various events, followed by the heading *FATAL ACCIDENT AT THE REGATTA*. In that article it is reported that measures were taken to safeguard the spectators, but at the same time, it seems that insufficient safeguards were in place to ensure the safety of those in close proximity to the cannons, in particular the children. The unfortunate Caroline apparently had no parental supervision and one wonders where were her parents at this time and why, after the Inquest and Ministerial Investigation was her body released to her 'friends' to arrange interment. There is no mention of her parents, George and Margaret Ridge.

According to the 1841 Census for Bedford, the young George Ridge was living in an institution, the Blue Coat Hospital, in the parish of St. Paul's. There were 18 girls and 19 boys between the ages of 9-13 years. The Blue Coat Hospital was in Harpur Street [The Bedford Directory and Almanac – and history of the town]. In 1831 this comprised a range of buildings, in the Tudor style of architecture, situated in Harpur Street. These buildings consisted of the Commercial [formerly the preparatory Commercial,] the General Preparatory, and the Girls' Schools, as well as a Blue-

Coat hospital for the board and education of poor boys and girls. George received an education at this establishment, and was obviously trained or apprenticed until he qualified as a tailor. It seems that children of poor honest parents, 'no bastards' and of good health attended the Blue Coat School (which was not a reformatory). They were given food, lodging, clothing and instruction. It is much the same as Christ Hospital Schools, which was an organisation set up for bright students from poor backgrounds. On leaving school George served his apprenticeship as a tailor. Perhaps bricklaying was more lucrative and this explains the change of career in later life. It can be concluded that he was a bright boy from a poor but honest family, fortunate to be educated and equipped for a trade or profession.

George married Margaret Carter on 24th December 1849 at Clapham, Beds, and the 1851 Census shows them living at Gravel Lane, Bedford. He is a tailor by trade. In 1857 Margaret gave birth to a son, William Ridge, who died aged 1 year 5 months and was buried on 18th June 1858. Also on 19th August 1857 the couple lost their five-year-old son George William Ridge, in tragic circumstances. At this time they are living in Harpur Street, Bedford. The 1861 Census reveals that they are living at 20 Harpur Street, The Albion Public House, with a son John aged 6 years and daughter Caroline aged 2 years. In 1867 Margaret had a third son, Charles Ridge, who died aged 1 year, in 1868. Their daughter Diana Caroline Ridge died in tragic circumstances, as already described, in July 1869. By this time George Ridge describes himself as a 'bricklayer'. It seems likely that Margaret ran The Albion public house.

In the 1871 Census for 20 Harpur Street, Bedford, the Albion public house, George and Margaret [having lost four children] have three remaining children, John aged 17, William aged 9, and George aged 5 years. Both George and his son John are bricklayers.

The Albion Public House

The *Bedford Mercury*, Saturday 29th August 1857 reported that a little boy named George William Ridge, aged 5 years, slipped into the river at the Common while playing on the bank. The family were living in Well Street, now part of Midland Road (near Specsavers) but where there was originally a well in the middle of the street hence the street name. The accident was observed by someone who ran to a boat which was a short distance away to alert the occupants, a man and a boy, what had happened. They lifted the deceased out of the water by using the sculls, and imprudently held him with head downwards 'to let the water run from him'. Having been undressed and rubbed down with a flannel, he was carried home to his parents, but he could not be saved and he died at 3 o'clock on Thursday morning. An Inquest was held at The Nags Head, St. Paul's and a verdict returned of 'Accidental Death'. Death was a frequent visitor to George and Margaret's home.

Having lost three sons, the last of these in really tragic circumstances, namely an unsupervised little boy of 5, playing on the river bank and slipping in to his death, one would think the parents would take steps to ensure that their children were safeguarded and not allowed out on their own, particularly by the river, but this was not the case and so Caroline's death followed. Only nine years after her death, on April 11th 1878, George Ridge her father died aged 47, at Bedford. In 1879 Margaret married her second husband Joseph Lowe. He was a shoemaker. Her son George aged 13 years was apprenticed to a shoemaker (presumably his step-father).

Margaret Lowe died in 1891 aged 60 years. On 13th April 1891 she transferred the licence of the Albion Public House to her son William Ridge aged c. 30 years and it remained in the Ridge family for 60 years. It may be assumed that son John was always a bricklayer, George a shoemaker, and that William had always helped to run the pub.

George was fortunate to be afforded a place at the Blue Coat School, and apprenticed to a trade which enabled him to support a growing family and to obtain a licence to run the Albion which also offered rooms for rent, bringing in a second income. All of the information we have concerning this enterprising and industrious family, still leaves unanswered questions about why their children were not better safeguarded, and in particular, why were the parents not present at the Inquest and the Magisterial Investigation and why was poor little Caroline's body released to her 'friends' rather than to her parents and family for burial. She was buried on July 19th 1869 and there is no memorial.

Rest in peace little Caroline.

Sources:

The Bedford Times and Bedfordshire Independent, July 20, 1869 p.5
The Bedfordshire Times and Independent, 18th April 1891
The Bedford Mercury, Saturday 29th August 1857
The Bedford Directory and Almanac 1831
Free BMDs: 1849, 1857, 1878, 1879, 1891
Census returns: 1841, 1851, 1861, 1871
Grave reference: 105 G-8 (4/126), date of burial 19.07.1869

Photograph:

Maurice Nicholson (source unknown)

SUICIDE OF A BOY

Henry Powers

What would induce a 15-year-old village boy to take his own life in the 1870s?

'On Thursday afternoon an inquest was held by Dr. Prior, borough coroner, at Mr. George Adams', the Crown Inn Britannia-road, on the body of Henry Powers (15), baker.

'Mr H. A. Dale, of the King's Arms, was foreman of the jury. The Rev. C. Brerton, St. Mary's, to which parish the deceased belonged, was present during the inquiry. The jury having been sworn proceeded to view the body, after which the evidence of Mrs. Powers, the boy's mother, was taken at her residence, the state of her health not permitting her to go out of doors. This was to the effect that at about six o'clock on Wednesday evening the deceased came in from work. She asked him to go to the bakehouse and get the ferment ready for his father. The boy replied, "Can I have my tea first?" Mrs. Powers answered - "No, that (the ferment) must be set, because it is an hour behind time." He then said - "I should like my tea." to which she replied - "If you can't do it I will." She set the ferment and deceased came into the bakehouse and helped her. Something then passed about deceased having had some beer at the brewer's, and witness went in and got tea ready. She sent for him to come to tea, but he sent word he should not.

'Some time afterwards her little boy Alfred Charles, went to look for deceased and found him hanging from a beam in the loft, his knees touching the straw. He called his mother who lifted the deceased, whereupon the rope came off.

'The remaining evidence was to the effect that the deceased had latterly been very irritable and could not bear children to touch him. He was from childhood not right in his head and frequently wandering if he was in the least poorly. He was generally of a reserved, sulky, moody temper. Mr. Johnson, house surgeon at the Infirmary, was at once fetched by William Smith, a neighbour, but though he tried all the usual means for endeavouring to restore animation he was unsuccessful. The jury at once returned a verdict to the effect that deceased committed suicide while in an unsound state of mind.'

This is a very strange case of a young boy described as a baker. There is no record of what Henry had done that day, only that he had come in from work. Could his depression have been caused by the pressure of work?

Bakers were to be found in every village and community at that time, sometimes more than one, all in demand and thriving. These were family businesses. One such character records his life-long experiences of working – and sometimes living – with a baker in the village of Wootton, from the time he left school:

'Having learned the trade, I spent all my working life at the bakery, working for this family, until my retirement. I'd make up a batch of dough in the dough trough, using a sack of flour, fifteen gallons of water, salt and yeast. It all had to be mixed up and left to "prove". The oven held 250 loaves and we filled it two or three times a day. The oven had to be set, and the coal fire stoked up. The furnace was filled about twice and then you knew when it was hot enough. We would throw in some flour and if it burnt quickly you knew it was ready. We used to make fruit cakes up on a Thursday, round ones and long ones, and these all sold. I'd do anything at the bakery including feeding the horses and deliveries off the cart. I learned my baking from Pa Juffs. People used to bring turkeys, geese and hens to us at Christmas, for roasting. We'd put less coal on for these and gauge the heat carefully. We used a smaller fire for lower temperature cooking, what we called a "fair heat".

'I've lived in Wootton all my life. Years ago I knew everyone in the Wootton area. It was all very quiet then. I used to go round Marston, Pillinge and Broadmead, Bourne End and Wootton delivering. On Good Fridays we made thousands of Hot Cross Buns and delivered them, also at the big houses – Wootton House and the vicarage. Ethel Pearce was the cook there, but she didn't make the bread. People had fresh bread delivered every day and paid nothing for the delivery. Apart from the three village bakers there was also one at Marston, Harry Lovell, and Mr Pulley from Cranfield.

'Mr Juffs kept livestock including pigs and cows, and horses for the delivery rounds. It was a thriving business.'

Frederick Burraway

William Juffs, Wootton Baker and Mealman, 1912

Perhaps this work was too great a challenge for poor Henry, described as being 'not right in the head'. Perhaps too much pressure of work and in conflict with his mother over his dinner and also his beer-drinking, caused him stress and despair, resulting in his suicide. Too much responsibility for a fifteen year old boy with emotional problems possibly. Tragic, whatever the circumstances.

Sources:

*The Bedford Times and Independent, Tuesday January 18th 1870 p.8
Bedfordshire's Yesteryears, Vol. 3, p. 25 Craftsmen and Trades
People, B. Fraser-Newstead*

DEATH THROUGH A BROKEN TOOTH

Maud Mary Robinson

The following article appeared in the local press in August 1899:

'An inquest was held at the King William Inn, on Saturday evening, before Mr Lucas, deputy-coroner for the Honour of Ampthill, to enquire into the circumstances attending the death of Maud Mary Robinson, a young girl 16 years of age, residing with her parents at Ivy Cottages, High-street, Kempston. The jury were Messrs Jos. Smith (foreman), Isaac Nelson, J. Robinson, M. J. Tory, H. Keep, F. Redman, A. Tory, J. L. Lack, J. Morris, F. W. Foster, F. Clarke and E. Mallows. After they had been sworn and the body viewed, P.s. Nicholls stated that the mother of deceased was too ill to give evidence.

'Elizabeth Huckle, who lived next door to the Robinsons, said she had known Maud for a number of years. She was healthy and strong as far as she knew until last October, when she had something the matter with her throat and nose. It came on gradually and got worse and witness noticed that she could not talk plainly, and her lips were bad and rather drawn up. She afterwards went as a patient to the Bedford Infirmary, and a few weeks ago witness accompanied her to the Convalescent Home at Hunstanton. She complained of her nose and throat whilst there, and was no better on her return. She was not in much pain, but her breathing was difficult and she had not walked about much.

'Mr Andrew Chillingworth, M.R.C.S., of Bedford, said deceased and the last witness visited him at his house on Friday week. He examined her ears and nose, and came to the conclusion that she was suffering from adenia, - a vegetation in the posterior of the nasal organs. She desired him to remove the growth, and he arranged to do so at her home on 28th ult [the last, ie 28 July]. On that date witness and his partner (Mr A. S. Phillips) administered chloroform, and the growth was successfully removed. About two minutes after the operation it was noticed that the patient suddenly turned blue and ceased to breath. They at once commenced artificial respiration, and freed the mouth from blood. The patient was then inverted, but as the breathing was very infrequent, tracheotomy was performed [opening of the windpipe] and artificial respiration kept up for an hour, but as there were no signs of life they were discontinued. On examining her mouth, it was found that the crown of the first molar tooth on the right side was missing and showed evidence of recent fracture. This would be the tooth on which the point of the gag which is used in these operations rested, and his opinion was that the tooth escaped into the throat, and this caused suffocation.

'Mr A. S. Phillips, M.R.C.S., said when he administered chloroform, about one and a half drams, deceased took it readily. The operation took about five minutes, throughout which her breathing was normal and her pulse good. When returning to consciousness the patient turned over on her left side and shortly afterwards turned blue; all their efforts to restore her were unavailing.

'The Coroner, in summing up, said the medical men had done everything in their power. From the evidence before the jury it was clear that deceased died from asphyxiation, caused by a tooth in her mouth being broken off by accident during an operation, and 'which became fixed in her windpipe, thus causing suffocation'.

'A verdict in accordance with the above was returned. Much sympathy has been expressed throughout the parish with the bereaved family.'

Poor Maud obviously suffered considerably and the surgery which should have resolved the problem appears to have been the cause of her death. What a sad loss of life of an otherwise healthy sixteen-year-old. Surely this should have been an avoidable accident and a likelihood the dentist would have been aware of?

The unfortunate Maud died on 28 July 1899 and was buried on 2 August 1899 in Kempston Cemetery.

The 1891 census lists Alfred Robinson, 41, Occupation miller's waggoner, Mary A. Robinson, 44, laundress, Annie L. Robinson, 14, daughter & scholar, Frederick C. Robinson, 9, son & scholar, Maud M. Robinson, 8, daughter & scholar and George Robinson, 1, son.

Sources:

The Bedfordshire Mercury Friday August 4 1899, p.5
Census 1891

A BABY BURNT IN ITS CRADLE

Maud Rogers

This next incident involves a baby girl whose life was cut extremely short:

'An inquest was held at the Bedford Infirmary on Monday – before Dr. Prior, the Borough Coroner, and a jury of which Mr. W. Wright was chosen foreman, - touching the death of Maud Rogers, the infant daughter of Samuel Rogers, butler, of Wootton Church End, who was burnt in a cradle on the previous Friday and died from the injuries sustained.

'Elizabeth Lovell identified the body of deceased.

'Mrs. Rogers, the mother of deceased, said that on the previous Friday she dressed the baby and put it in the cradle, which stood about half a yard from the fire, in front of which was a large guard. A night-shirt and a sheet hung on the guard to air. Witness went up-stairs, leaving her little three-year-old girl on the hearthrug in front of the fire. Hearing the baby cry, witness went down stairs and found the cradle in flames, and she noticed the burnt remains of the sheet and nightdress on the guard. Witness snatched up the baby and wrapped it up in her dress, and put out the fire with some water.

'The child's wounds were dressed by Mrs. Foster, of the Vicarage, and the baby was brought to the Infirmary in a conveyance. Witness could not account for the origin of the fire, but she noticed a piece of burnt paper in the fender, and probably this was ignited by a fallen cinder and set fire to the clothes. Her little girl was not in the room when she got downstairs, and she was not in the habit of playing with fire.

'Dr. Skelding, house surgeon at the Infirmary, said the deceased was brought to the institution on Friday afternoon suffering from severe burns on the head and arm. She was in a state of collapse and died the following day.

'Ex-Inspector Haynes, the Coroner's officer, said he had been to the house and saw the guard, which was a heavy iron one, two feet high, and it was impossible for the little girl to have reached over or through it to the fire.

'The jury returned a verdict of Accidental Death.'

This does seem something of a mystery; how it happened was not revealed at the time and never will be, but it is such a sorrowful event and would have been devastating for the child's mother.

Source: The Bedfordshire Standard, Saturday December 21 1889 p.6

A BOY DROWNED

Thomas Rose

Here is just another tale of a small boy losing his life in the River Ouse:

'Dr. Prior, Borough Coroner, conducted an inquest at the "Woolpack," Commercial-road, on Monday morning at noon, touching the death of a boy named Thomas Rose, who was drowned near the old Water Bridge late on Saturday night. Extravagant rumours were about during Sunday to the effect that the lad had been pushed into the water by Italians, but the evidence adduced [brought forward] at the inquest made it clear that he was throwing another boy's dog from the bank, trying to teach it to swim, when he pitched forward and was drowned without anyone knowing, save another little chap who was with him but who appears to have run off home in fright.

'Mr. Joshua Grant was foreman of the jury.

'Lucy Jordan, a married woman of 1 Butcher's Yard, St. Mary's, said that deceased had been living with her for the past three years. He was 12 years of age last October, and used to go to school. She last saw him alive at 4.45 on Saturday night, when he started on an errand for her to a coal merchant's in Gwyn-street. He did not return, and witness became uneasy. Her husband and the boy's little brother went to look for him, but could not find him. About 11.20, however, the latter came home with the truck deceased had taken, stating that he had found it against the Embankment steps filled with coal. She then communicated with the police and asked them to drag the river. In answer to Mr. W. G. Johnson, witness added that deceased could not swim; she did not believe he had ever been in the water in his life.

'Charles Howe, a schoolboy, aged 7, living with his grandmother in Dame Alice-street, was the second witness. He could not tell the Coroner what book a testament was when he was handed one, and was therefore not sworn. He said he went with Tommy Rose down the Embankment steps with his dog. They left the truck on the top. Rose took hold of the dog by its collar and "throwed it in the water so as it could swim." He fell himself, and looked as if he swam a little way on his back. He went down then, and witness thought he told a big boy before he ran home.

'Inspector Setchell said that on Sunday, about 12.20 a.m., he was on duty at the Police-station when Mrs Jordan came there and reported that a lad who was lodging with her, had been missing since 5 p.m. He questioned her, and she said he had a crippled brother who had gone to St. Albans and who would be home between 2 and 3 o'clock that morning; it was possible he might have gone to meet him. Witness told her to let the police know directly this brother came home whether the lad really had gone to meet his brother. She came to the station again shortly before 3 a.m., and said the brother had come home but had seen nothing of the deceased. In the meantime witness had instructed all the constables on night duty to be looking out for the boy, but up to that, 3 a.m., they had found no trace of him. After Mrs Jordan had called the second time witness heard that the boy's truck had been found on the Embankment, and he then considered advisable to drag the river. In company with P.c. Fensome, he proceeded to do so in the vicinity of the steps near the Old Water Bridge, and pulled up the body the first time he threw the drag in. Mr W. G. Johnson came to the scene and ordered the removal of the body to the mortuary.

'Mr W. G. Johnson deposed that he examined the body of deceased soon after 3 a.m., lying on the steps of the Embankment. The lad was fully dressed, but quite dead. His hands were firmly clenched, and his eyes wide open; there were all the usual appearances of death by drowning. Later on witness examined the body again in the mortuary, and found two marks at the back of his head, one on each side, as if the lad had struck some hard substance in falling, or in floating on his back as the boy Howe said he had done.

'Mr Haynes, Coroner's Officer, told the jury that as far as he had been able to ascertain, the boy Howe accompanied the deceased right from Gwyn-street to help him push his truck of coals, and they were followed by the dog.

'The Jury found a verdict of "Accidentally Drowned."'

Thomas had 'lodged' with Lucy and Henry Jordan who is listed in the street directory as a 'labourer' and in an earlier directory as a 'blacksmith'. They lived at the time of the accident at 1 Butcher's Yard, St Mary's. It appears a little odd that a nine-year-old boy would be lodging with a family other than his own; could this be a case of informal fostering?

Butcher's Row c. 1899

According to the 1901 Census, the family, living at 36 Tavistock Place, comprised Henry Jordan aged 46, born in Bedford, and described as a 'shoeing smith' but over-written 'black' his wife

Lucy Jordan aged 47 and born in Souldrop, and their son Leonard Jordan. There were three borders, Frederick Rose aged 19 and a general labourer, Albert Rose aged 17, a cycle-maker's assistant, and Florence Boase a two-year-old. The next-door neighbour is listed as Frederick Boase and his 24-year-old daughter Ellen Boase.

The 1891 Census shows a child born 1886 (November or December), Thomas Gerald Rose; this is presumably the child known as Thomas Rose.

Steps at Old Water Bridge (see also page 93.)

Sources:

The Bedfordshire Times and Independent, 9 December 1898 p.5
Grave ref. Section B.383
Buried at Bedford Cemetery on 8 December 1898 aged 12
There is a second burial in this grave on 19 March 1971, Trixie Beatrice
Harper aged 73. There does not appear to be a headstone.
Birth certificate for Thomas Gerald Rose dated 1886 Ref. 3B327
Census: 1896, 1891, 1901

FATAL ACCIDENT AT THE AMPTHILL ROAD SCHOOL

Annie Louise Ward

It is unusual to hear of a child's death occurring at school, but it did occur locally in 1889:

'An accident, unhappily ending fatally, occurred at the Ampthill-road Elementary School, on Nov. 20th, the victim being a little girl named Annie Louise Ward, the daughter of a corn and coal merchant in Cauldwell-street. It appears that during the customary break shortly before eleven o'clock, the deceased and other girls were playing "tick" in the schoolground, and the deceased with a view to escaping from being ticked, jumped on to the boundary wall which is surmounted by an iron railing. The stone coping of the wall is bevelled and the deceased in running along it overbalanced and fell over the rail on to the ground. She did not then appear much the worse for the fall and continued her lessons during the morning, but next day she was not so well, and medical advice was called in by her parents. However the skill of the doctor was of no avail to save her life, and the poor girl died on Nov. 28th

'The inquest was held on Saturday morning at the Angel Inn, Cauldwell-street, by the Borough Coroner (Dr. Prior), and the following jury:- Messrs. G. Evans (foreman), W. Sadler, W.

Wright, J. Lenton, W. Horne, C. Hockliffe, G. Setchell, G. Frost, G. Rubythorn, W. Griffith, B. Creed, J. Dudley, and C. Bumstead.

'After the body of the deceased had been viewed, the following evidence was adduced:-

'Edward Ward deposed that the deceased was his daughter, and that she was nine years and eight months old. On Wednesday, Nov. 20th, at half-past eight o'clock in the morning, she left home to go to the Elementary School, and returned about 12.30 complaining of a stiff neck, but did not say that she had met with an accident. The next day she appeared to be worse, and Mr. Johnson was summoned. The deceased was then questioned as to an accident having befallen her, but only made a rambling statement. She was at times insensible, and continuing to grow worse, died on Thursday afternoon, Nov. 28th.

'Clara Hare, a little girl, deposed that she went to school with deceased, and was in the same class. On Nov. 20th at a quarter to eleven o'clock they went into the playground and had a game of "tick" over the rails. The deceased stood on the stone-coping of the wall, and in trying to avoid the other players, she fell headfirst over the railing, alighting on the ground in a doubled-up condition. She got up and went back into school, but whilst she was doing her lessons she complained of feeling sick.

'Emily Bowler, another school-girl, gave corroborative evidence.

'Mr. W. G. Johnson, surgeon, said he was called to see the deceased on the previous Thursday week. He found there was brain mischief, but she died from peritonitis, probably her liver having been injured by the fall. She was insensible at the time of her death.

'The Jury returned a verdict of "Accidental Death."'

Ampthill Road School opened in 1876, funded by the Harpur Trust. It subsequently became a Board School, and under the control of the Council from 1903. From 1973 it was known as Raleigh Lower School and sadly it closed in 1995. The photo of the school was taken in 1945 showing the decorative Victorian and rather grand building, which still remains.

Annie, whose home was in Cauldwell Street, St Mary's, Bedford, was buried in Bedford Cemetery on 2 December 1889, aged 9.

Aerial photo showing Ampthill Road School

Sources:

Died 28 November 1889, Buried in Bedford Cemetery 2 December 1889 aged 9
Grave ref: F.657.
EAW021847 ENGLAND (1949). Ampthill Road, the W.H.A. Robertson & Co Ltd Lynton Engineering Works and environs, Bedford, 1949. This image was marked by Aerofilms Ltd for photo editing.

Photograph:

Maurice Nicholson

DEATH FROM BURNING, WILDEN

George Simpson

According to the local press, the incident reported here occurred in Wilden on March 12, 1887:

'On Friday an inquest held at the Bedford Infirmary, before Dr. Prior, Borough Coroner, touching the death of George Simpson, aged 16, who died on the previous Wednesday from burns he received by falling in the fire on February 19, at his home at Wilden. The following were the jurors: - Messrs. W. Gurney (foreman), A. White, Arthur Harrison, James Beattie, George Baines, W. Stuart, Joseph Kasteliner, William C. Walters, Jas. Bonser, Joseph Joyce, Henry Johnson, and George T. Brandon. The following evidence was taken:

'Annie Simpson said she was the daughter of Wm. Simpson, and lived at East End, Wilden. The body shown to the jury was that of her brother, George Simpson, who lived at home and was 16 years of age. Deceased was subject to fits, which came on suddenly, and he had one about every four months. On Feb. 19 last he was at work for Mr. Thomas Smith, of Wilden, and about half past nine at night came home, having been waiting to see his master. He was sitting by the fire, having his supper, when he had a fit and fell in the fire. Witness was in the room at the time, and pulled him off the fire as quick as she could. He fell on his hands and witness ran and fetched Mr. Bennett. There was no one in the room but witness, and the fire was in the grate. -

'William Bennett, labourer, of Wilden, said the deceased was well-known to him; he was a fairly intelligent youth and capable of any sort of farming work. He had known him to have fits on one or two previous occasions. On Saturday, Feb. 19, about 9.30 p.m., the last witness went to his house and said that her brother had had a fit and had fallen in the fire, and that she had pulled him off. Witness ran immediately, and found deceased lying on the floor; he was still in the fit and convulsed. After some time his father came and they got him in a chair, when they found his hand had been burnt. Witness got a trap, and deceased was taken to the Bedford Infirmary. He had known deceased to work at several places.

'Mr. Sydney Robert Alexander, house surgeon at the Infirmary, said the deceased was taken into the institution on Feb. 19, about midnight, and was suffering from a burn on the right hand, and of part of the fore-arm; he was quite sensible, and he was treated in the usual way. Deceased went on well till the end of the month when tetanus [an acute infectious disease usually occurring through a contaminated wound] came on and, getting worse, he died during a paroxysm [any fit or convulsion] on March 2, the cause of death being primarily a burn and secondly tetanus.

' A verdict of "Accidental death" was returned.'

What a terribly sad case of a vulnerable young person losing his life tragically, in his own home. This accident may well have been prevented had the fire been guarded and it is surprising that no-one anticipated the danger in view of his tendency to fit. Sad too, that in his condition he had to work on a farm, with heavy and potentially dangerous machinery. He may well have had epilepsy throughout his life and that in itself is an awful burden to carry.'

Sources:

The Bedfordshire Standard, Saturday March 12 1887 p.3
Collins English Dictionary

SERIOUS GUN ACCIDENT, BARTON

Thomas Sturgis

Loaded guns present severe hazards when irresponsibly left in public places, and it is not surprising, perhaps, that on this occasion in 1887 a young teenage boy lost his life as a result.

'A fatal accident through incautiously playing has occurred, at Barton. It seems that at the beginning of last week a gun had been obtained from the Rectory Farm (Mr. Osborn's), in order to shoot a troublesome rat, but as it could not be got at the gun was returned, and placed in a stable. On Tuesday evening the lads employed on the farm, began larking, and the gun was picked up by a lad named Pearce, and aimed at Thomas Sturgis, a lad, thirteen years old, son of Charles Sturgis, a labourer on the farm. Pearce pulled the trigger, and to his astonishment the gun went off, its charge entering Sturgis's left shoulder and making a ghastly wound. At the moment Sturgis was stooping to scrape the mud off his boots. The shot smashed the shoulder bone to a pulp, and made a mass of lacerated flesh intermixed with his clothing.

'Dr. Muncaster was called and gave the poor lad stimulants to restore him from the shock. In the meantime information of the accident was sent to Dr. D. Thompson, of Luton, and preparations were made for the lad's reception in the cottage hospital.

Amputation of the arm and part of the shoulder was found necessary, but the case was hopeless, and the lad died from shock to the system about one o'clock on Thursday afternoon.

'The inquest was held at the George Hotel, Luton, on Friday, before Mr. Whyley, County Coroner, Mr. F. Croft acting as foreman of the jury, who returned a verdict of "Accidental Death."

The funeral took place at three p.m. on Sunday, when the church was crowded to overflowing. A wreath, composed of lovely white chrysanthemums, and different kinds of ferns, sent by Mrs. Cornwall, was placed on the coffin by the Rector. Wreaths were also brought by Mr. Walter Osborn, Miss Martha Cook, Ernest Hook, and William Hodge, the latter three having been closely connected with the lad in the Sunday school. On reaching the grave, the hymn, "Brief life is here our portion," was very impressively sung by the church choir and the assembled throng. The body was also followed to the grave by the Sunday school teachers and scholars, and many who had come out of respect to the deceased.

'At the evening service, a very impressive sermon was preached by the Rector, the Rev. J. F. Cornwall based on Ecclesiastes xi., 7-10, and xii., 1-7, - "The preacher touchingly alluded to the life and death of the lad, who had been a member both of the choir and the Sunday school. The hymn, "A few more years shall roll," was sung immediately before the sermon, and "Days and moments quickly flying" after the sermon. Mr Walter Osborn, employer of the deceased, has been most kind and liberal to the parents; he has borne all the expenses incurred by the funeral and otherwise, and shown the greatest sympathy in the whole affair.'

It appears that some inter-denominational conflict occurred during the planning of the funeral for this most unfortunate young man. The Vicar refused permission for hymns to be sung by the Wesleyan choir at the funeral. Thomas was a member of the choir and attended the Wesleyan Church Sunday School. More details can be found in the local press.

Source:

Bedfordshire Standard, Saturday November 26, 1887, p.8

INQUEST ON A CHILD BURNT TO DEATH

Charles Henry White

This article, which relates to a little boy aged only three years and two months, appeared in the *Bedfordshire Times and Independent*, Saturday 31 December 1881, p. 6.

'An inquest on the body of Charles H. White, who died on Friday of last week from the effect of burns, was held on the following morning, at the Flower Pot Inn, Tavistock-street, before the coroner, Dr. Prior, and a jury consisting of Messrs. J. Cook (foreman), J. Tysoe, G. Ward, R. Barker, B. Powers, J. Connor, T. Fletcher, G. Hulatt, J. Banks, G. Covington, J. Powell, A. Corby, and J. Kemp.

'The jury having examined the body.

'Evidence was given by George White, aged 26 engine cleaner/fireman employed on the Midland Railway, father of the deceased, and residing at 28 Queen-street, showing that the child, who was three years and two months old, was seen by him alive and well at 4.30 p.m. on Thursday, the 22nd inst. [instant, a moment in time]. On returning home from his work at 10.15 the same night he found that the boy had been extensively burnt. Dr. Adams was present and had just finished dressing the child. Deceased, however, got gradually worse and died at 11.15 a.m. on the next day, having previously told his father that he had burnt his toes by putting a piece of paper into the fire.

'Emma White, mother of the child, who was very much distressed, stated that on Thursday she put her boy to bed with his brother. She had to go into a neighbour's house, taking her baby with her. In twenty minutes she returned to the house, and on opening the door perceived a strong smell of burning. Going upstairs she found articles of her boy's wearing apparel lying partially burnt on the stairs, and in a room she saw her child lying on the bed very badly burnt. The child told her that he set fire to his toes with a piece of paper, but she had no doubt it was his nightdress which caught fire. Before she went out there was a lamp on the table, but it was not lighted, and on returning she found it on the table just as she left it.

'By the Jury: The child was not in the habit of getting out of bed to come downstairs.

'Dr. Adams stated that on Thursday night at about 20 past nine he was summoned to Queen-street, and he was on the spot by half-past. He was told that the messenger had been to two other medical men, but they were not at home, and the police ordered him to get the first doctor he could find. Witness found deceased lying on the bed, on his right side, all covered up except his head. The whole of the body was burnt excepting the feet, and parts of legs, back, and right side. The hair was singed, and there were extensive burns on the body, chest, hands and back, which were quite denuded of the scart skin [the outermost layer of the skin]. He applied the usual dressings with the aid of his assistant, Mr. Eastwood. After being there an hour and a half, witness left just before eleven, considering the case a critical one. Burns of that extent on a child so young were necessarily fatal. At eight the next morning he was told that the child was worse; he went to see it and ordered what he considered necessary, but it was apparently sinking, and the child ultimately died in the collapse stage which usually lasted about two days.

'The Coroner, in summing up, pointed out that mothers must go out sometimes and leave their offspring, but every precaution should be taken for the protection of the children from injury. In this case the jury should consider that the mother had stated that, before leaving the house, she closed the stairs-door, set the paraffin lamp on the table and put it out; and on returning she found that the lamp had been untouched.

'The jury returned a verdict of "Accidental Death," and requested the Coroner to privately caution the mother against leaving children in her house under dangerous circumstances, this being meant as a warning to others who may be following a similar practice.'

One wonders why the doctor did not send the child immediately to the Infirmary, and regarding his visit the following day he should have been asked what he "considered necessary"; in the many cases of serious accidents I have encountered in my research, I have yet to read of painkillers having been given and that bothers me. Concerning the child's mother, nothing can be more important or urgent than attending to her child and safeguarding it. There was no need for her to leave her child alone and she should have been severely reprimanded for doing so, in my personal opinion.

How ironic that the father was a 'fireman' and his child was killed by fire (from whatever source).

This couple – George 26 and Emma White, aged 24 and lacemaker– were married for 52 years (married in 1877) and in that time in a 20-year period, they had ten children: Charles was born in Elstow, as was his brother William born 1880 and died 1881, Others were Elizabeth, George, Albert, Alice Maud, Catherine May, Florence Emily, Sarah and Joseph. Their father George died in 1929 aged 74. They were living at 28 Queen Street, Bedford.

According to the 1891 census the family were living at 9 Ford End Road, Bedford and he was described as Engine Driver. They had a boarder, a Retort Setter (they lived opposite the gas works). Daughter Sarah and Joseph 3 were living with them.

We next find them living at 8 Marlborough Road, with George still an engine driver, and Emma listed as 'wife'. William aged 21 was a boot repairer, Elizabeth a dress maker, son George a moulder and Albert an errand boy. Catherine, Florence and Sarah were scholars, and Joseph 3.

Sources:

The Bedfordshire Times & Independent, 31 December 1881, p.6
Buried 27.12.1881 in Bedford Cemetery
Grave F10 112
Census returns 1882, 1891

CONCEALMENT OF A BIRTH

Baby Weston

This is a lamentable tale of the death of a newly-born baby girl and the subsequent trial of the parents, Agnes Weston and Henry Gilbert, in August 1891.

Agnes Weston was indicted and on bail for concealing the birth of her illegitimate child on August 10th and appeared at the Bedfordshire Assizes on Saturday November 21st 1891. At the trial Mr Bonsey prosecuted and Mr Harris QC defended. Whilst on bail Miss Weston left Bedford to spend time with her family in Wiltshire, returning to stand trial on 21st November; she also spent a month at the Bedford Infirmary during this period.

Agnes Weston was a 22-year-old cook and domestic servant, single and in service, employed by Mr Leggatt who lived at Sunnyview, 23 River Crescent, 'Gwyn-street' near the Embankment in Bedford. There were ten people altogether in the household, Mr and Mrs Leggatt, their two sons and two daughters, a governess, Philip Heisch, brother-in-law, Rose Currington, house and parlour maid and domestic servant and fellow servant Agnes Weston. Rose and Agnes lived at their place of work, where they shared a bedroom. Prior to August 8th Rose, a witness at the trial on November 21st 1891, noticed that Agnes was enceinte [French pregnant] but had not commented on this. On the morning of August 9th Agnes asked her to get the breakfast and Agnes then came downstairs at 8.30 am, when she fainted and went to bed; she returned to bed twice during that day. In the evening Agnes was given leave to go out and returned about 10 and went to bed. The following morning Rose woke about 5 and saw Agnes leave the room with a foot-bath full of linen and carrying her shoes in her hand. After breakfast the prisoner told her she had a mishap on Sunday morning and Rose saw a sheet in the copper which Agnes had washed. On Monday evening Agnes went out and borrowed Rose's mackintosh. When she came in Rose made her bed and noticed only one sheet, doubled (she elaborated on the state of the bed at trial). On the Wednesday Agnes told her that she had hidden the child's body in a copper on her master's premises and then locked it in her box during the Sunday and took it out on Monday evening to Harry who threw it in the river, and that was why she wanted her mackintosh. Harry was her 'young man'. Although the time-scale is somewhat confusing, there is no doubting the outcome of Agnes's actions.

Detective Gordon confirming that he went to the prisoner at the house in 'Gwyn-street' to explain to her that she would be arrested, also said that two days previously [on 24 August] he and Sergeant Setchel had dragged the river and recovered the body of a newly-born child wrapped up and tied with string and copper wire to a brick. It was after his visit to her that she left Bedford and returned to Wiltshire. It was stated that the prisoner 'left the house on Friday'.

Dr Phillips stated that he opened the parcel and found no marks of violence whatever upon the body of the child. He examined the child and also confirmed that there was no evidence that the prisoner had given birth to a child but there was evidence of a miscarriage; he queried whether evidence of a birth was required for a conviction for concealment following a birth. He stated that 'certainly there was no evidence of concealment'. This is very odd indeed.

Rose knew of Agnes's condition since March but did not tell her mistress. Agnes was apprehended on [August] 26th and charged. On the 24th [August] Rose had seen a parcel containing the body of a child pulled out of the river near Mr Leggatt's house, and she pulled out a piece of mackintosh. P.s. Setchill deposed [witnessed in a court of law] to dragging from the river the body of a child. The same day he examined the prisoner's bedroom and in her box found a bottle labelled 'steel drops'. [Steel Drops are still available and are advertised as 'a good source of iron']. Discussion ensued and Mr Harris submitted that there was no case, there being no evidence that the prisoner had had a child but only evidence that she told Rose Currington so. Mr Bonsey said if the jury believed Rose Currington they must convict the prisoner.

Mr Harris pointed out that the prisoner had made no attempt to conceal the matter from the fellow servant and that concealment of the body did not amount to concealment of birth. However, in summing up the judge said there was clear proof that the girl had given birth to a child and there was her own statement that she had locked it in her box. He stressed that if they were satisfied with Rose Currington's evidence they must find the prisoner guilty. The jury then retired to consider their verdict.

The prisoner was found guilty but the jury strongly recommended her to mercy.

The judge said because Miss Weston had given every information to the authorities, he would – under these circumstances - take a very lenient view of the case, and his sentence would be that she would be discharged from prison to come up for judgement when called upon. This was received with loud applause at the back of the Court.

Henry James Gilbert was similarly indicted for concealing the birth of the illegitimate child of Agnes Weston at Bedford on August 10th. He pleaded not guilty. Mr Bonsey opened the case and said that although girls were often charged with concealing the birth of their illegitimate children it was unusual for their seducers to be placed in the dock on a similar charge and although the sympathy of the jury would be naturally enlisted on behalf of the girl, he did not think there was much room for sympathy for the man who was the cause of her trouble.

Rose Currington gave similar evidence as with the previous case and said she knew the prisoner kept company with Agnes Weston. P.s. Setchell said on August 24th he saw the prisoner who said to him 'Do you want me?' and they went to the police station. The prisoner subsequently made a statement that one night Agnes Weston came out of Mr Leggatt's house and gave him a parcel which they took to the recreation ground; they both tied a brick to the parcel and she sat on the form while he threw the parcel in the river near the overshot. The prisoner directed the witness [P.s. Setchell] to the spot and he recovered the parcel from the river. The proceedings continued and the *Bedfordshire Mercury* reported as follows:

'Agnes gave him a parcel one night outside Mr Leggatts' and they went down to the river over the Suspension Bridge, to the Duck Mill meadows, near the back of the over-shot. She sat on a form and helped him to tie up a parcel; she still sat there whilst he went and threw it into the river. In answer to a question by the Inspector, he said that he knew that she had been ill and he had reason to know what was the matter with her. Afterwards Gilbert went with them to the spot by the river, showed them where the girl sat, and where he threw the parcel in. Detective Gordon commenced dragging, and they soon brought up a parcel to which was attached a red brick, on which Gilbert said, "By God, you've got it." On being charged, the prisoner signed a statement admitting that he received a parcel from Agnes Weston, that they then went to the river, and he threw it in.

'Detective Gordon corroborated part of the evidence of the Police Sergeant, and added that the prisoner had said he had offered to marry the girl in March.

'Dr. Phillips was again called, and stated that he opened the parcel and found no marks of violence whatever upon the body of the child.

'Mr. Harris, addressing the jury for the defence, contended that the man did not know that the parcel contained the body of the child. There was no doubt, according to evidence, that it contained the body, but there was no evidence that he knew it. It might have been a foetus or some other matter that she desired him to throw into the water. Prisoner had acted perfectly straight in the matter, and there was a good deal to be said on his behalf.'

In summing up, his Lordship pointed out that the very fact of concealing the body was a crime and if such a thing were allowed it would be a strong temptation for hundreds of illegitimate children to be murdered. If the prisoner assisted to put the body in the river that was a secret disposition but he also commented that according to his statement the witness 'seemed to have done all he could to undo the wrong he had committed'. He stated that 'In all of these cases, which unfortunately were not rare, there was a great temptation on the part of those concerned to get rid of the body at any costs, and it required a great moral courage on the part of the girl to stand up against the approbrium of public disclosure'.

Mr Harris stated in his clients' defence, that Gilbert had offered to marry the girl but she declined, and that 'both were very respectable'. The girl had come out of the infirmary that morning and the affair had nearly killed her. When they heard the police had got the matter in hand both gave themselves up directly.

The chaplain of the Bedford Infirmary said Agnes Weston had been there a month, and had expressed sincere contrition for what she had done. His Lordship thought that in the circumstances the jury were justified in recommending both prisoners to mercy.

After some deliberation the jury found the prisoner guilty and hoped the judge would deal leniently with him.

Agnes Weston and Henry Gilbert were both discharged and

told they were to come up for judgement when called upon. This decision was received by the public in court with loud applause.

This intriguing and horrifying case resulted in a charge for failure to declare a birth; one might well ask why it was not a trial for manslaughter or murder. After all, the child [a girl] was born alive. Perhaps the outcome of a trial for manslaughter or murder would have resulted in a charge of guilty followed by an appropriate sentence to fit the crime. Some might take a more sympathetic view of a young girl pregnant and frightened of the shame and humiliation about to be inflicted on her family and herself in addition to the prejudice and possible ostracism her child would face being illegitimate. The fear of revealing her plight to her employer would have been substantial, leading to loss of position, poverty, degradation, persecution and worse, and the actual birth and the actions she took following that birth must have terrified her. Perhaps she contemplated abandoning the child but clearly it was not her intention to do so. Agnes faced the terror of delivering her own child and what followed illustrates that she had sufficient strength to deal with the situation alone.

Following the birth Agnes may not have been physically well or in a normal state of mind; she could have suffered post-natal depression (known then as puerperal insanity). This in itself could have led to an act of infanticide. Agnes's child died very soon after birth however. It is not known when her employer became aware of her plight and when he did, whether he offered any support. The fact that no marks of violence were found upon the body of the child, does not exclude, for instance, death by suffocation. After all, the concern seems to have been directed at failure to declare a birth, not investigating murder or manslaughter. Little wonder that Agnes showed 'severe contrition' whilst in the Infirmary.

It is interesting to note that some of the blame was apportioned to the man by the court, and not just to the woman, which is unusual for the 19th century and a male-dominated society. Some would maintain that Agnes was one of many young women who found themselves pregnant whilst unmarried, but who could not be described as bad. At the age of 33 she was still in service as a cook, and unmarried, perhaps deterred from marriage by her experience of having a child out of wedlock, and the dreadful outcome of that situation.

This whole affair unfolds dramatically; it has the power to leave the reader shocked, appalled and incredulous. The child is the unnamed, unloved, unregistered victim whose only crime was to be born illegitimately. Some may consider that what followed was a 19th century 'honour killing' as horrific as any our modern-day society has known. Was there a thorough inquest on the child's body; was she given a Christian burial; is there a grave and headstone? It seems the only record of that sweet helpless unfortunate child – of whom there is no visual image – is the trial of her brutal parents. The couple have been described as 'respectable' but surely in 1891 or 2021 and at any point in between, no person disposing of their newborn child by dumping it weighted in the river can be described as respectable. There was no way of undoing this dreadful wrong that had been perpetrated. The lenient sentence resulted not in public disapprobation it seems, but in a vulgar round of applause. *The Bedfordshire Mercury* used the heading A Merciful Judge but this innocent little child was sadly shown no mercy whatsoever.

The records show that Henry James Gilbert born in 1865 and aged 26 at the time of the incident and   indictment, went on to marry in the autumn of 1901 and the 1911 census shows him and Rhoda Robinson Gilbert nee Bayes living in Kempston with son John Henry.   As for Agnes it appears that she engendered sympathy in court – as did Henry – with their lenient sentences and the applause which greeted their release.   This outcome surely sent a message to other women in a similar situation, that they could destroy a life with impunity and walk free.   Agnes could have avoided this debacle by marrying her lover in March when she realised that she was pregnant; Rhoda Bayes accepted his offer of marriage in 1901 and we know that they were together with a son, ten years later.   Some would say that because of her decision to decline marriage to her baby's father Baby Weston died in vain and that subsequently this sad little child was denied the right to life.

Henry James Gilbert was buried at Foster Hill Road cemetery on 5th January 1931, aged 66 years.   The address was recorded as St Peter's Hospital, St Peter's, Bedford.   Grave reference Q.715.

Agnes Weston was born in 1867 in Devises, Wiltshire.   The death register indicates that Agnes Weston spinster died in 1950 aged 83 at Rotherham; no other references have been found.

Baby Weston was buried at Bedford Cemetery, Foster Hill Road, Bedford.   The age was recorded as 'a few minutes'.   The child is buried in an unmarked grave and the burial took place on 27th August 1891. The name is recorded as 'Female Child of Agnes Weston'. A Memorial to 'all our babies' is visible in the distance behind the burial plot, bearing the inscription *(see also page 24)*:

IN REMEMBRANCE OF ALL OUR BABIES
SO DEARLY LOVED
"AND HE TOOK THEM UP INTO HIS ARMS
AND BLESSED THEM"

St Mark Chapter 10 Verse 16

The opinions expressed in this chapter are the Author's; others may disagree. However we interpret these events, surely far more sympathy is due to the child than to the parents?

Agnes did not marry and had no other children. She must have been haunted by the episode through her life.

Sources:

The Bedfordshire Mercury, Saturday November 21, 1891 p.6
The Bedfordshire Standard, Saturday November 21, 1891 p.6
The 1891, 1901 and 1911 census
Baby Weston's Grave ref. A.885
The burial record entry is No. 860 and is on page 172 of Register No 11
Henry James Gilbert's burial record is grave Q715

SUDDEN DEATH OF A CHILD

Baby Savage

This is yet another heart-breaking story of the death of an illegitimate baby boy soon after birth.

'On Thursday evening, Mr. E. Eagles, jun., the coroner for the borough, held an inquest at the White Horse public-house, touching the death of a male child to Lucy Savage, a single woman living in White-Horse-street.

'It appeared from the evidence of Sarah Renshaw, a married woman, that Lucy Savage was on the previous morning, about half-past ten o'clock, confined of a male child, Mr. Crick, herbalist, of White-Horse-street attending her, and being present at her confinement. The child looked healthy when he was born, but it slept all through Wednesday, and several times changed black in its appearance, when Mrs. Renshaw, who was the only attendant on the mother, took it to the fire and warmed its feet. Mr. Crick went in twice during the day, and he was informed of the circumstance but he expressed his opinion that there was nothing the matter with the child. It was fed on arrowroot during the day, and Mrs. Renshaw remained with the mother during the night, the child appearing very restless and frequently "squeaking" out. The coroner particularly enquired of Mrs. Renshaw whether the child had had any medicines but she distinctly denied that it had. About eight o'clock on Thursday morning the child "squeaked out" and Mrs. Renshaw went to it; it drew one breath, and then died. She immediately ran out to Mr. Crick and told him she was afraid the child was dead. She observed at the time of its death that it had a dark appearance.

'The Coroner (to Mrs. Renshaw): It appears a strange thing to me that you didn't send for a doctor at all.

'Mrs Renshaw said they had no idea that the child was ill.

'Mr. Charles Robinson, jnr., surgeon, stated that he had examined the body of the child that morning, and he observed a blackness of the lips and finger nails with a slight construction of the finger and thumb. There were no marks of violence, and he believed the child died from natural causes.

'The Coroner said that he had the power of requesting a medical gentleman to make an examination and to state to him whether there was anything wrong, he should not have troubled the jury at all; but as the holding of an inquest was the only way of disposing of the matter, he had thought it right when it had been reported to him that a healthy child had been born and that it had died without any medical attendance, to summon a jury together. As there had previously been some excitement in the town with reference to cases only Mr. Crick had attended, he had thought it would be better, for his (Mr. Crick's) sake that there should be an inquiry of this kind. It was not usual when children were born apparently healthy for them to die, as this had done, and if such cases were allowed to remain open, there would no doubt in a short time be a great number of children disposed of.

'The jury agreed with the remarks of the learned coroner, and returned a verdict of "death from natural causes."'

There had indeed been 'some excitement' in the town with reference to cases only Mr. Crick had attended, and this is evidenced by an article which appeared in *The Bedford Times* on Saturday, March 19, 1859 entitled Alleged Manslaughter by a Herbalist. A trial was held at Bedfordshire Summer Assizes when William Francis Crick, 41, medical botonist, of Harpur-street, Bedford, was placed at the bar and indicted for the manslaughter of Henrietta Mobbs, an eight-year-old child of St. Cuthbert, Bedford, on the 1st of January last. After considerable hearing of evidence and debate, the jury were asked to decide whether the child died from the remedies she had been given (by a chemist and Mr. Crick), and not from the disease. Unless they were satisfied of that they were bound to acquit the prisoner. The jury immediately returned a verdict of NOT GUILTY. The judge (his lordship) addressed the prisoner thus: "You should be cautious in future how you make use of these medicines, for that they are of powerful character in the opinion of the witnesses who have now given evidence."

The prisoner responded "My Lord, the witnesses have said they found lobelia in the medicine. I now state that there was not a particle of lobelia in it at all." The prisoner was then ordered to be discharged.

A doctor, Richard Dennis Hacon M.D. 'surgeon practising in the town' examined the child after death and gave the cause of death as peritonitis. In his analysis of stomach content he found lobelia, cloves, and capsicum. Dr. Hacon considered that it should not have been prescribed.

Dr Hacon was called on the evening of 27 December to see the body of the child. He saw it on the next morning.

Perhaps Mrs. Renshaw was unaware that although Mr. Crick was not convicted of causing the death of a child, there must be some doubt, given all of the evidence. Perhaps she was also unaware that the child could have been taken to Bedford Infirmary (opened in 1803 for the treatment of the poor), where he would be treated by a qualified practitioner and would no doubt have survived. Just another sad loss to the town and community of Bedford and quite possibly an avoidable death.

Sources:

The Bedford Times, Saturday, March 19, 1859
The Bedfordshire Mercury, Saturday, October 1861

CONCEALMENT OF A BIRTH AT STEWKLEY NR LINSLADE

Baby Foster

On March 6, 1896 *The Bedfordshire Standard* reported a most shocking discovery:

'The recent discovery of a child's body in a Well: -

'Minnie Foster, domestic servant, aged 22 years: belonging to Stewkley, Bucks, six miles from Leighton Buzzard, who appeared in discharge of bail, was charged at the Linslade Police Court, on Monday morning, before Major Finlay and Mr. B. T. Fountaine, with concealment of birth. The case arose out of a discovery a fortnight previously of the body of an infant wrapped in a cloth in a well on premises occupied by a man named Faulkner, at Stewkley, and at an inquest held by Mr. F. T. Tanqueray, coroner, it transpired that the child had belonged to the prisoner, and that the body had been kept in a box for some days after birth in London, and then brought to Stewkley, and, after the lapse of a further fortnight, put down the well.

'At the inquest evidence was given by Mr. Johnstone Harris, a medical practitioner, that the body was too much decomposed and generally broken up for it to be possible to say whether the child had been born dead or alive. The prisoner herself stated that it was born dead, and the jury returned an open verdict.

Prisoner's statement, as read on Monday, was that in July last she had been staying temporarily at her sister's house in Kentish Town, London. She slept in her sister's front room, alone, and the child, of which she had not expected to be delivered for a month, was born dead during the night. She wrapped the body in a cloth, put it in her clothes box, and said nothing about it, but stayed with her sister another fortnight, and then went home to Stewkley, taking the body with her in the box, and ultimately putting it down the well, where it remained from the middle of August until the middle of last month.

'Mary Sharp, the prisoner's sister stated that when she came to her in London she appeared to be unwell, but when asked as to her condition, gave an evasive reply.

'The prisoner, who on Monday made no further statement, was committed for trial at the Bucks. Assizes, but re admitted to bail.'

On March 13, 1896, p.6 *The Bedfordshire Standard* (Letters to the Editor), published the following article:

The National Society for the Prevention of Cruelty to Children

'Sir,

'Will you kindly permit me through your columns to correct what appears to be a widely diffused impression with reference to the recent Bazaars held for the Society, which impression is seriously affecting the income of the Society for its daily work throughout the land. Large sums have been raised by these Bazaars and wide circulation has been given by the press to this fact, and since then the ordinary income of the Society has gone down nearly 25 per cent. This has placed the Society in great straits for its current work on behalf of the 2,000 suffering children per month brought to its knowledge. The Bazaar fund goes wholly to reserve. The Society therefore earnestly appeals to people, anxious to help it in its vast and beautiful work, for generous support. The Treasurer is the Hon. Evelyn Hubbard, M.P., 7, Harpur–street, London, W.C. Cheques should be crossed Bank of England.'

BENJAMIN WAUGH,
Central Office, 7, Harpur-street, London, W.C.
6th March, 1896

It is good to know that charities at the time were actively engaged in preventing child cruelty, but those children born out of wedlock were the most vulnerable of such children and one wonders what steps were being taken to support those babies and their unfortunate mothers.

Source:

The Bedfordshire Standard, Friday March 6, 1896 p.9

SAD DROWNING FATALITY

George Harold Greenough

Another child drowned in Bedford in April 1896:

'Mr. Mark Whyley, coroner for the County, attended at the Irrigation Farm, Bedford, on Tuesday afternoon, to hold an inquest touching the death of George Harold Greenough, a lad aged nine, of Pilcroft-street, Bedford. On the previous afternoon some boys, including the deceased, were playing on Newnham Bridge, when the deceased tried to get at some palm in the river. For this purpose he stood on the pole which is chained to the bridge, but slipped and fell into the river. Mr. Flood was chosen foreman of the jury.

'Dr. Rowland Coombs stated that on the previous afternoon he was sent for to the Irrigation Farm to see a boy who had been taken from the river and who was supposed to be dying. He came and found the body of deceased lying in front of the fire. He was quite dead, and he should think he had been so quite half an hour. He examined the body and found no marks of violence upon it, but the appearances were consistent with death from drowning. The man who was in charge of the body told the witness that he had made prolonged efforts to restore animation, but without success.

'Albert Ernest Greenough, cabinet maker, of 70, Pilcroft-street, father of the deceased, said the boy was nine years old, and he last saw him alive at Monday dinner time. He went to the Ampthill-road Elementary School, but it was holiday time. As witness was going over the New Bridge someone asked him if he was looking for his little boy, because he was dead.

'John Perkins, a boy aged 12, living with his mother at 30, Cardington-road, Bedford, said he went to the Ampthill-road School, and the holidays ended on the previous day. He went in the Duck Mill Meadows to play, and the deceased got on to the scaffold pole, which was chained on to the bridge to stop the boats from going under. He was there for the purpose of getting some of the palm out of the river, but he slipped and fell into the river back-wards. Witness further explained that the deceased was going to get on to the bridge, and for that purpose had got one foot on the pole and one on the bridge when he fell backwards. After he had been under the water once they tried to get him out with a stick, but could not reach him. He did not splash nor call out. When they found they could not get him out they shouted, and Mr. Hills came. He did not strike his head on the pole or bridge, but fell quite clear of it. When Mr. Hills came he dived in after him.

'Alfred Bird, aged 10, of Pilcroft-street, corroborated.

'Mr. I. Hills, engineer at the Irrigation Works, said on the previous afternoon, in consequence of what his daughter informed him, he went outside and jumped in the river and got the deceased out. He laid him on the bank and tried to bring him round by artificial respiration, but it was of no effect, and at no time did he show any sign of life. The depth of the water would be about 6ft. 6in., and the deceased was about forty yards from the bridge.

'The Coroner, having summed up, commented on Mr. Hills' heroic conduct and suggested to the jury that they should add a rider to their verdict.

'The jury returned a verdict of accidental death, and added a rider as suggested, complimenting Mr. Hills on his heroic conduct.'

Source:

The Bedford Standard, Friday April 1896 p.7

A BEDFORD YOUTH DROWNED AT CASTLE MILL

Robert Charles Smith

'On Saturday afternoon, June 23rd [1866] considerable excitement was occasioned in Bedford by the intelligence that Master Robert Charles Smith, second son of the late Robert Smith Esq of Bedford, had been drowned in the River Ouse, near Castle Mills, in the parish of Goldington. The melancholy accident occurred shortly after 2 o'clock, and although every available effort was made to recover the body, the means employed were not successful until about eight o'clock in the evening, - by which time the body had been in the water about six hours.

'The deceased had gone with several of his school-fellows to Castle Mills for the purpose of fishing and bathing, and the manner in which the accident occurred and the noble efforts of Master Walter Palmer to save the life of the deceased, are detailed in the subjoined evidence. Great praise is due to Mr Roe of Bedford for his promptness in driving over with the drags and men immediately on receipt of the sad intelligence. The exertions of the men engaged at the mill, and Mr Purser jnr Of Willington in diving for the body, of Mr James jnr of Cople, - of police constable Haynes, - and the readiness of Mr Palmer of Willington, and Mr Charles Rogers of Castle Mills in drawing off the water, as well as Capt Polhill-Turner in kindly granting the use of his small boat, - were all of them most praiseworthy.

'Arrangements were made for holding the inquest the same evening, in order that the body might be removed to the residence of the mother of the deceased – Mrs Tregenza of St Cuthbert Street, Bedford, - before Sunday.

'By nine o'clock a most respectable jury had assembled at the Swan, Goldington, when the Coroner for the county (Mark Whyley, Esq) took the following evidence:-

'Walter Palmer swears: I live at 6 Lansdowne Terrace, Bedford. My father is a commercial traveller. I knew the deceased. I overtook him at Castle Mills. We went to bathe in the river. My brother John Archdale was there. He called out to me that the deceased was in danger. I swam as fast as I could to the place. He caught hold of me round the waist with his arms and legs. I managed to get him about twelve yards off the land then I got free from him and got to land. This was about two o'clock. It was a wide part – the bottom part of the locks. Frederick Smith and some other boys were there with us. The brother of the deceased went for the miller. He came almost directly. I stopped for about a quarter of an hour and then went to Goldington. I went back to the place and saw the body of the deceased taken out about a quarter past eight o'clock, by police-constable Haynes. The deceased could swim a little. We were fishing. I think the deceased merely swam out of his depth.

'Police-constable Haynes sworn: I am a police-constable at Bedford. I was sent for this afternoon by Mr. Roe About 4 o'clock to assist In finding the body of deceased. I dragged for some time. I then left and obtained a boat. I eventually got the body out about five minutes before eight o'clock. I saw the body taken to the Swan, at Goldington. The body viewed by the jury is the body of the deceased, Robert Charles Smith.

'Dr Coombs sworn: I am a medical man residing at Bedford. I was sent for about three o'clock at
castle Mills. I went and remained some time whilst attempts were made to recover the body. I have seen the body at the Swan at Goldington. I know it to be the body of Robert Charles Smith. I have made an external examination of the body. The appearances presented are perfectly natural. There are no marks of violence. I am of opinion that the immediate cause of death was drowning.

'George Pruden corroborated the evidence of Walter Palmer.

'The jury immediately returned a verdict of "accidentally drowned."'

This was a sad loss of a 12-year-old boy, and not the last young person to be lost to the River Ouse. Robert was buried in Bedford Cemetery on 27 June 1866 next to his brother John William Smith who died aged 5 years and 7 months on 20 May 1863 and was buried 25 May 1863 and his father Robert Smith who died aged 52 and was buried 10 December 1862. Robert's gravestone reads:

In Affectionate Remembrance
Of
Robert Charles
Second Son Of
Robert And Esther Smith
Of Bedford
Who Was Drowned Whilst Bathing

On The 23rd June 1866
Aged 12 Years

"O When the First Wild Throb is Past
Of Anguish And Dispair
To Lift The Eye Of Faith To Heaven
And Think My Child is There
This Best Can Dry The Gushing Tears
This Held The Heart Relief
Until The Christian's Pious Hope
O Becomes A Mother's Grief"

Robert was part of a rather large family. The 1861 census shows them living at 25 Adelaide Square, Bedford. The head of the family, Robert Smith is described as a 'landed proprietor'. His wife Ester Smith is 37, the children are Samuel H Smith aged 10, Mary Smith 9, Robert Charles Smith 7, Leonard C Smith 6, all described as 'scholars'. John/James William Smith aged 3 [died aged 5 years 7 months in 1863], Henry Smith aged 1, Frederick Smith aged 1 and Sidney Herbert Smith 4 months [died age 5 in April 1866]. There were two servants.

There was a twenty-year age gap between Robert and Ester; all of these children were Robert's. After his death in December 1862, records show that Ester re-married. The wedding took place on 12 January 1865 at St Cuthbert's Church, Bedford, of John Tregenza and Ester Smith [Bedfordshire Mercury, 14 January 1865]. John Tregenza, auctioneer, had been Councillor of West Ward in Bedford in 1862.

Sources:

The Bedford Mercury 30 June 1866 p.8
Grave Reference: Robert Charles H.4. 10, his brother John William
H.4. 20 and father Robert H.4.30 (no headstone)
Died: 23.06.1866 and buried 27.06.1866.
1866 Bedford Directory

FATAL ACCIDENT TO A BOY

Samuel Cookson

It was in May of 1882 that the local press reported on a fatal accident which occurred on the Midland Railway, in which a young boy lost his life. This is the original article:

'An inquest was held before Dr. Prior, borough coroner, at The Corn Exchange, on Thursday morning, on the body of Samuel Cookson, aged 15, who was killed on the Midland Railway under circumstances detailed in the evidence. The Jury were Mr. T. Hague (foreman), Messrs. W. Coote, G. Walton, A. Wicken, S. Sharman, W. Smith, H. Maclin, T. Whitworth, J. Mays, J. Bucks, S. Groom, E. Bush, and W. Cockerell.

'John Sergeant, printer's apprentice, 8, St. Cuthbert's Street, identified the body lying in the Mortuary as that of Samuel Cookson, who was also an apprentice with him at Mr. Walsh's. On Tuesday evening at 8.45 they were together and coming from Poplar Avenue, with a view to getting on the Avenue Road. John Bailey was also with them, and they were out for a walk. They crossed the line at the level crossing near the bridge. Bailey and witness got over the line, and Cookson was caught by a train from Manchester. He saw the buffer catch him, and after the train had gone witness found the boy lying on the line between the four-foot. Bailey pulled him off the line and laid him on the path at the side. It was getting dusk and they could not clearly see his condition. His clothes appeared torn all to bits, and they could see that his legs were off.

'P.s. Pedley here produced a catapult which he found in deceased's pocket.

'Witness said he had seen Cookson use the catapult and shooting into the river with it. He did not know whether Bailey had one; witness had not one with him. The train looked a long way off when he called out to Cookson to stop, but Cookson made no reply.

'Mr Kinsey deposed that between 12 and 1 a.m. on Wednesday he was called to the Mortuary to see the body of the deceased. The head was crushed and only attached to the body by about an inch of skin; the arms and legs were cut off, and death was instantaneous. The injuries were such as would be inflicted in the manner described by the last witness.

'John Bailey aged 16, employed at the Ordnance Survey Office, said he accompanied deceased and Sergeant on Tuesday evening. They had been to Poplar Avenue, and were returning by the line when the train came up. Witness got across and did not see the engine strike the deceased. He picked up the body and laid it at the side of the line; he noticed that the head and legs were off. Witness had a catapult with him but he did not remember using it; Cookson used his a few times, but not to shoot at the trains. He did not see Sergeant with a catapult.

'The Coroner and Jury expressed their opinion that the witness must know whether he used his catapult or not, and it would be much better for him to answer yes or no.

'Bailey adhered to his statement that he could not say whether or not he did use his catapult.

'John Peacock, labourer, in the employ of the Corporation, stated that on Tuesday night he was at the Anglers' Rest when he heard an alarm that an accident had occurred on the line. Witness and others hastened to the spot, accompanied by one, Papworth, who gave the alarm, and found the body lying on the up side of the line. A stretcher was procured, the body was put into a brake, [a light carriage] attached to an engine, and witness assisted to convey it to the mortuary.

'The Coroner said the evidence was clear enough, and the duty of the jury was plain. The boys were undoubtedly out on a mischievous expedition, and probably they were after the jack [rabbit or hare] in the ditches.

'A verdict of "Accidental Death" was returned, Bailey was called in and advised as to his future conduct.

'Mr. Potter, Inspector for the Midland Company, said several engines which passed the spot about the time mentioned were examined, but no blood was found, and none of the drivers knew anything about it.'

The Bedford Midland Railway Station opened in the 1860s and the line with its magnificent steam trains, would have attracted much interest in the area. Children are known to have been drawn to it, not appreciating the potential for accidents whilst at play. In the 1970s when the Writer was employed as a teacher in a Bedford school, children were repeatedly warned about the dangers of playing near the railway lines, particularly as holiday periods approached. It is to be hoped that with electrification of the lines, high speed trains and public awareness, railway accidents and fatalities among children at play have diminished or have ceased to occur.

The tragic death of Samuel Cookson, still a child, and the impact on his grieving family having lost their son and in such tragic circumstances must have been devastating. According to the 1881 census, the boy and his parents Sarah and Richard Cookson were living at 46 Hassett Street, Bedford. There had been another son, Harry, born in 1872, baptised on 7 August 1872 but died and was buried in Bedford Cemetery on 28 August 1872 aged only ten weeks. Samuel was born on 2 March 1866.

Little is known of Richard Cookson except that he worked as a warder at Bedford Gaol. He does not appear on the 1871 census as being at home, and a check reveals that he was not on the Bedford Gaol entry for that night (2 April 1871) either, so obviously not at work. What is known is that the well-known executioner William Calcraft, is listed in the census as being at the prison, as a prisoner named William Bull was due to be hanged at 8 am the next morning. Perhaps Richard Cookson was at his post at the prison that day, 3 April 1871,when the first execution to be held at the prison hidden from public view, since the last public hanging in 1868 (of William Worsley) took place.

Some of my readers with a keen interest in social history, may wish to read the account given by the local press of the procedures leading to the execution of William Bull, convicted of murdering an elderly lady. This is reproduced in the following chapter.

As for the unfortunate Samuel Cookson, it is known that he attended the Harpur Charity School in the centre of Bedford. The school register for 1873 confirms this and gives his date of birth as 2 March 1866. His burial in Bedford Cemetery took place c. 13 May 1882.

Sources:

The Bedfordshire Times & Independent. Saturday, 13 May, 1882 p.5
1871 and 1881 Census
Burial Record grave reference G.10. 245
Date of death 9 May 1882
Buried 13 May 1882, aged 16
Foster Hill Road Cemetery Plan
Harpur Charity School Register, 1873

THE EXECUTION OF WILLIAM BELL

Monday Morning, April 3, 1871

The Bedford Times and Bedfordshire Independent, Tuesday April 4, 1871, reported that:

'The scaffold, which is the same structure on which Wm. Worsley was hung [in 1868 and the last hanging in public], was erected in the south-west corner of the premises immediately inside the front gate, and in order to carry out to the fullest extent the spirit as well as the letter of the recent Act of Parliament, the Governor had taken the precaution to put up a large screen from wall to wall, so as to shut out any possibility of being overlooked from the vicinity of the property in Adelaide-square. The scaffold was undraped and in its naked hideousness presented an appropriate accessory of the scene about to be enacted on its floor.

'At a quarter to eight o'clock the prison bell began tolling, as did also the bell of Holy Trinity Church, in accordance with instructions issued by the Home Secretary to the effect that the bell of the nearest church should be tolled on such occasions. In five minutes more the officials of the prison were marshalled in procession, and bearing black wands [rods], along the corridor leading to the front door of the gaol.

'At five minutes to eight the Governor of the Prison, and Calcraft, the executioner, who had arrived in Bedford on Sunday evening, entered the condemned man's cell. Bull was then led out, passively and quietly, to the landing outside the chapel door, and here he sat on a stool while the process of pinioning his arms was gone through by Calcraft. The convict's cap was then taken off, and remained on the floor beside the seat.

'The condemned man was then led by the executioner and by the Governor down the stone staircase leading into the front corridor, and now the procession to the scaffold commenced. The chief warder led the way, followed by four warders, two and two, with black wands. The chaplain, the Rev. J. J. Row, came next in order, clad in surplice, and repeating prayers audibly though with visible emotion. After him came the convict, supported on either side by a warder, and looking pale and careworn, though not presenting the wretchedly haggard aspect which was exhibited by Worsley at the last execution on his way to the gallows. The surgeon (Mr. Couchman), the under-sheriff (Mr. T. L. Hooper) and the governor of the prison (Mr. R. E. Roberts) followed abreast, and after them came the remaining officers of the prison, the rear being brought up by the representatives of the press, who were present on behalf of the public, and to whom every attention was shown by the Governor.

'As the procession issued out of the front door the convict was noticed to be deeply moved, and tears coursed freely down his cheeks. His step was, however, firm, and he betrayed no other signs of weakness or emotion. Judging from his subsequent behaviour it was almost impossible to resist the conviction that the tears he shed on the way to the place of execution were those of penitence and not of mere physical or mental depression.

When, however, he caught sight of the scaffold, his firmness gave way and he tottered a little but soon recovered his composure and went on.

'On the procession entering into the area in which the engine of death was erected, four warders ascended the scaffold, taking up their positions severally at the corners. Two mats were placed on the ground at the foot of the steps ascending to the platform. On reaching this part, the convict knelt on one, with the chaplain beside him on the other. The chaplain then, in a voice faltering with emotion, but with intense devotional earnestness, recited a brief prayer.

'The condemned man bowed his head with reverential lowliness during this terrible moment, and when the prayer was concluded he rose, with some firmness, and exclaimed audibly - "I feel thankful for all that's been done for me. I feel pardoned! Tell my mother." Thus his last words and his last thoughts on earth were about his mother, a touch of nature which the most revolting brutality cannot entirely efface from the human heart!

'And now the convict, shaking hands with the Governor and with the Executioner, ascends the scaffold. His steps are still firm, but there is a woe-begone expression on his countenance, tenfold intensified within the short interval during which he was walking from the front entrance to the fatal scene. He is placed on the trap, and we noticed that he then gave a look upwards towards the sky as if to take a last glimpse of it before his death.

'In a moment more the white cap is drawn over his face by Calcraft, who then adjusts the noose around his neck. The halter is then hooked onto the chain from the cross-beam, and the convict's feet are pinioned [bound]. The bolt is then drawn, and William Bull, the murderer of Sarah Marshall, is in the act of strangulation! The fall seemed to have an instantaneous effect, the only motion, except that inseparable from the unwinding of the rope, being a slight muscular action in the hands, which as death was supervening [an after event], relaxed the firmness of their devotional grasp, and moved backwards and forwards convulsively. There was little or no oscillation of the legs, and manifestly death had quickly relieved him from his sufferings, if, indeed, he was conscious of any after the fall of the drop. The surgeon remained on the spot until life was extinct, and then the group around the scaffold retired into the prison.

'Immediately upon the execution being completed, a black flag was hoisted in front of the Prison as an indication to the assembled crowd who lingered outside, that the last penalty of the law had been carried into effect. The representatives of the press were then taken into the Governor's office, where Mr. Roberts placed in their hands the following:

CONFESSIONS,
Condemned Cell, Bedford Gaol,
5.46 p.m., 20th March, 1871

'Statement Voluntarily made to the Governor in the presence of one of the Warders:

'I got home that night about half-past ten, I am sure it had not gone eleven. I had had a little beer but was not drunk. I do not know if I had a fair trial. I did not take much notice of what took place. I was satisfied with the Counsel that defended me. I admit the justice of my sentence. I threw a stone at old Sally's door and she opened the door and swore at me. I stood in the middle of the road at the time – it was said so. I could not see if Sally was in her night dress, there was no light in the house. She stood at the door for five minutes swearing at me. I cannot say she knew me. She kept swearing at me until I went into the house. As soon as I got in she called me a "hen roost robber." She was then standing in the middle of the room; but I do not know if she was dressed or undressed. I was only two or three minutes in the house. After the stone was thrown she came out to the stile, a long sweeping broom in her hand. She struck at me with it, and the head of the broom came off near the stile. She picked it up and went into the house. I followed her, and she struck me one or two times. I never saw green that night, and it is so long ago now I do not know what to say; the last time she "hot" me I knocked her down with my hand; I was in a rage with her. She was lying on the bricks when I left the house and was swearing at me; she was not dead. I never meddled with the bed. Sally was not on the bed while I was in the house. I never used a stick, as was spoken about. I had no criminal action with her; all I did was to knock her down, and when she was down I "hot" her the second time.''

Robert E. Roberts, Governor
James Bettles, Warder

William Bull was a Labourer, aged 21. Sarah Marshall, his victim, was 52. She is described as an "imbecile woman" in the press reports, and it was known that she was often tormented by youths in the village of Little Staughton, where both she and William Bull lived - he with his mother. This particular incident took place on November 29th 1870.

There is a great deal of information in the press concerning the incident, and it was reported that "her throat had been violently pressed, (and that) her death was caused by suffocation." Other details are given but her death was officially recorded as being "caused by strangulation" and it was clear that a violent struggle had taken place. This conflicts with the Statement given by William Bull. [*The Bedford Times and Bedfordshire Independent*, Tuesday, March 21, 1871 p.6].

Much detail was withheld until after the execution to avoid attracting too much public attention and the "morbid taste of a portion of the public which seeks its gratification" (in obtaining as much information as possible concerning the convict). A crowd of mainly women, estimated to be 700 gathered outside the prison in the early morning on the day of the execution, only dispersing after the flag was flown.

William Bull was spared the humiliation of a public hanging. It is hard to believe that anyone would wish to observe a public hanging but this was the case until the parliamentary decree which terminated public executions c. 1868. Not only was the execution observed by many in the past, but also commemorated in lace bobbins (and other objects no doubt) used by so many women throughout Bedfordshire in the 19th century. These bobbins were often made of ox bone and were engraved with the name of the deceased and date of execution. It would be interesting to know how many of these survive.

Samuel Cookson's father Richard, being a warder at the prison, may well have been on duty at the time of this execution and participated in the proceedings. If so he must have been equally perturbed and affected as it appears were those involved and who witnessed the sad event.

Richard Cookson lost another child, a boy born in 1872 and who died in August 1872 at the age of ten weeks. The picture shows the proximity of Bassett Street where the Cookson family lived, to the prison where Richard worked.

Image from 1928 showing Bedford Prison top right and 46 Hassett Street marked with a cross

(https://britainfromabove.org.uk/)

Sources:

Bedford Times and Bedfordshire Independent, April 4, 1871, p.8
Bedford Times and Bedfordshire Independent, March 21, 1871, p.6

Photograph:

Courtesy M Nicholson (source unknown)

CONCLUSION

I have illuminated the lives and deaths of some of the children researched but there must be many more yet to be discovered. It is necessarily difficult to ascertain the precise circumstances in which infants lost their lives. Illegitimacy reflected badly on the women themselves and their families and because of prevailing prejudices and poverty in society, steps were frequently taken to terminate, conceal or destroy the evidence. Mothers often took on a daughter's illegitimate child as their own, concealing the reality from those outside the family, the child's birth mother becoming the 'sister'. Those who found an alternative husband willing to take on their child were indeed fortunate, but for the least fortunate the Workhouse was often the last resort. Children labelled bastards were tarnished and shunned through no fault of their own.

The photograph shown overleaf of Paradine Court off Harpur Street and next to the new 'B and M' store, illustrates the extremely poor conditions in which impoverished people resided. Street Directories show that there were 13 dwellings in this small Court and the occupations listed over a short period of time include Labourer, Hawker, Blacksmith, milkman, milk-seller, shoemaker and bricklayer. Most of the lone females listed do not appear to have occupations. Such poor living conditions were not conducive to large families and the well-being of infants and young children in particular. This is an extreme example of poor living conditions, but I suggest poverty may have been a factor in the deaths of some of the children whose story I have related.

The Bastardy Laws stretch back as far as the 16th century, when the Parish in which the child was born sought to trace the father and oblige him to marry the mother. Failing this he would be held responsible for financial support until the child could be apprenticed. The alternative was the Bastardy Bond whereby a relative, friend or benefactor assumed that responsibility, to ensure that upkeep did not fall on the Parish (and community members).

Paradine Court

Deaths of older children were the result of a variety of circumstances but it does appear that the majority of these children met their fate in the River Ouse. Attitudes to child welfare were far more lax than now, but children are never entirely safe even today however observant and careful the parent.

The Foster Hill Road Cemetery is a beautiful place to visit, a typical Victorian cemetery with fine statuesque memorials, simpler structures for those of less affluent means and no memorials for many, especially children. The ancient trees, documented and revered comprise many magnificent specimens, an Orchard is in its infancy and flowers provide colour and tantalizing scents throughout the flowering season. I urge you to take a quiet and calming stroll; through the rustle of the leaves and the stirring of the summer breezes you may hear whispers down the corridors of time, and feel the presence of the children with whom you have now been acquainted. Lend a sympathetic ear to their voices from beyond. Be moved by the sweet summer fragrances, the glorious dappled sunlight, the wonderful solitude. Enjoy the atmosphere, sounds and splendid contentment, the nostalgia and delights that life offers us.

Brenda Fraser-Newstead

Source:

The Bedford Directory

Photograph:

Courtesy M Nicholson

Printed in Great Britain
by Amazon

24946541R00165